Faery Magick

Spells, Potions, and Lore
From the Earth Spirits

by Sirona Knight

New Page Books
A division of Career Press, Inc.
Franklin Lakes, NJ

FAERY MAGICK

EDITED AND TYPESET BY KATE PRESTON
ILLUSTRATIONS © 2003 KATE PADDOCK AND *WWW.ARTTODAY.COM*
Cover design by Lu Rossman/Digi Dog Design
Printed in the U.S.A. by Book-mart Press

To order this title, please call toll-free 1-800-CAREER-1 (NJ and Canada: 201-848-0310) to order using VISA or MasterCard, or for further information on books from Career Press.

The Career Press, Inc., 3 Tice Road, PO Box 687, Franklin Lakes, NJ 07417
www.careerpress.com
www.newpagebooks.com

Library of Congress Cataloging-in-Publication Data

Knight, Sirona, 1955-
    Faery magick : spells, potions, and lore from the earth spirits / by Sirona Knight.
       p. cm.
    Includes bibliographical references and index.
    ISBN 1-56414-595-6 (pbk.)
       1. Fairies. I. Title.

BF1552 .K55 2003
133.4'3--dc21
                                        2002038946

Contents

Introduction

The faeries are the sacred spirit or presence that animates and enlivens all of Nature. Their knowledge, wisdom, and supernatural powers can be called upon when doing magick. Faeries create a field of resonance or vibration just beyond the spectrum of our ordinary awareness. They are one step away from our reality, normally just out of our range of perception.

The faery realm mirrors the mortal realm. Faery land is the home of our emotive primordial links with our origins, the home of universal wisdom and truth. To fully comprehend the concept of faeryland, the Otherworld of the faery, you need to view reality as layered (realm upon realm), rather than linear. In this sense, faeryland is everywhere–within and around you. It is ever-present.

Celebrated throughout history in several forms, faeries are among the most well-known magickal beings of all time. With the advent of the New Age, faeries have become even more popular and noteworthy. There are scores of faery books, movies, cartoons, television programs, and faery music. There are faery mouse pads for computers, faery e-cards, and faery screensavers. Faery artwork can be seen on posters, prints, wall calendars, magnets, and Yule tree ornaments. They appear on coffee mugs, jewelry, and even wedding cake toppers. You can purchase faery garden figurines, faery musical water fountains, faery garden balls, switchcover plates with faery designs, as well as faery toys, games, dolls, puppets, cookbooks, and chess sets. There are selkie bath salts, pixie dust powder, and faery apparel for children with flower faeries and whimsical frog and butterfly faeries.

Rather than being a primer on the faery tradition itself, this book is more a hands-on guide on how to see, attract, and communicate with the helpful faeries themselves. Working with the faeries is a creative and productive way for balancing a world precariously out of balance by caring and communing with Nature spirits. For the purposes of this book, I use the term "faery" as it is the traditional name of the bright people. I do not use terms such as the Little People, as most of the faeries I have encountered are not small or tiny, but human size or larger.

You can befriend faeries even if you cannot see them. They are one with all plant life as each and every living plant has a faery or fae within it. By communicating with your plants, you are communicating with the fae. The faeries will tell you what the plant needs and what the plant can be used for. Your intentions, expectations, desires, and depth of your merge with the helpful faery energies will determine the depth of your communication. If you respectfully ask the faeries, they will be overjoyed to co-create and play with you as is so magnificently exemplified in famous faery gardens of Findhorn and Perelandra.

Whether you live in the forest, suburbs, or the inner city, the faeries will greet and help you. The reason children hear and see the faeries more often than adults may be that they are more open-minded, pure of heart, honest, and steadfast of will. You know you have faery sight when you feel as if someone is watching you, but no one can be seen. Or you may feel as though butterfly or bird wings flutter next to you without touching you. Or you may suddenly smell a heady flower fragrance, see plants and trees glowing and shimmering with a fine light, or hear hushed giggling or soft laughter. Because the faeries are always near us and usually listen and watch us without being seen, it is always wise to speak well of them.

For the purposes of this book, I recommend that you plant a Faery Magick garden in spring during the month of May. If you plant the following flowers and herbs, you will have most of the fresh ingredients you will need to do the spells in this book:

* Basil.
* Chamomile.
* Daisies.
* Hollyhocks.
* Honeysuckle.
* Jasmine.
* Lavender.
* Marigolds.
* Mint.
* Nettle.
* Pansies.
* Red verbena.
* Rosemary.
* Sage.
* Strawberries.
* Thyme.
* Vervain.
* White, yellow, and red roses.

When working with the faeries, it's important to remember that all things are one, whatever they might be. Everything, including faeries and mortals, is made of the same stellar stuff—from star seed. Your physical body is halfway between the mortal and faery worlds, somewhere between instinct and spirit. Parts of you exist within the very body of the planet, in the trees, plants, and flowers. To be a complete being, you need to integrate your mortal and faery aspects. Working the spells in this book will bring you closer to that realization.

Faery History, Mythology, and Folklore

"When the first baby laughed for the very first time,
The laugh broke into a thousand pieces,
And they all went skipping about,
And that was the beginning of faeries."
–Sir James M. Barrie, Peter Pan

Journey: The Enchanting Voice

From outside my window in the early morning hour, I hear a voice that calls out in a beautiful, melodious voice. I slowly rise from my soft, warm bed, and step toward the window. As I do, I step beyond the bounds of my physical reality. I step beyond myself, stretching my awareness into another realm and reaching out to my full potential.

As my mind moves from a light sleep to full consciousness, I am suddenly aware of the enchanting quality of the voice I hear. I stare out the window for a few minutes, mesmerized by its cadence, before getting on my clothes and going out to explore the origins of the enchanting voice.

As I walk outside, the crisp morning air caresses my face, and my skin tingles. I walk down a gravel driveway that winds toward the general direction of the inviting voice. As I walk, the voice seems to envelop and surround me, making it difficult to determine where it is coming from. The dawning light of the sun is just becoming visible, and the pine and oak trees loom like giant shadows all around me. Rather than feeling menacing, they seem like giant protectors, standing guard along the way.

Upon reaching the end of the gravel driveway, I see the dark outline of a small path that leads downward into the vegetation that grows quite thickly together, making traveling impossible except on already traversed pathways. As I move down the path, I am greeted by the musty smell of the forest floor. I take a deep breath, and as I exhale, I become increasingly aware that the enchanting voice is louder and calls me ever closer, like a beacon of another world.

Further down the pathway, I smell water. I hear the tinkling of a creek. The sound of the water seems to provide background accompaniment to the enchanting voice. Although there is a path, I still have to make my way through the dense undergrowth that grows under the thick canopy of trees.

As I continue through the undergrowth, I can sense Nature all around me in her inherent splendor and divinity. The farther I walk, the more I become one with the Natural beauty around me. I pause to say a short prayer of thanks to the sacred land. As I walk on, the voice is clearer and closer.

Finally, I reach a shallow creek with a small waterfall that flows over white blocks of milky quartz crystal. I stop to rest and to get my bearings. In the still shadowy world of the early morning, I see a small greenish-blue creature stir within the waterfall. At first I think I am seeing things, but contining to watch, I instinctively know that what I am seeing is Nature faery, in particular a Water sprite.

For the flicker of an instant, time seems irrelevant and out of focus and the moment becomes an hour. Looking into the eyes and listening to the enchanting voice of the waterfall faery, I realize that the faery is the underlying spirit of Nature, in all its many aspects. The faery element in everything is that which gives spiritual life and beauty.

Sitting next to the waterfall, I look into the faery's eyes and I see my reflection. I see my ideal self, my beautiful and compassionate self. I also glimpse past and future life-times, flowing from the same spiritual well. The world I enter seems familiar, but there is something very different. Like looking in a mirror, I feel I am seeing everything reversed. My perception and awareness seem altered.

As I stand hearing the enchanting voice in all its splendor with Nature, the greenish-blue faery eyes meet mine and I can suddenly imagine living my life to its fullest potential. I imagine miraculous things like world peace, cures for all disease and illness, and a kinder, gentler world, where life seems more fluid and exciting and people are more tolerant. I feel a peaceful, easy energy washing over my body like the waterfall. This feeling empowers me and I feel at one with myself, with the water faery, and with the world around me.

In my life, the enchanting voice represents a calling that leads me back home. Like a salmon moving back up stream to spawn, I feel propelled to seek out my roots, and get a feeling for who I really am. While growing closer to the land around me, I realize my roots have something to do with the energy of the fae, who traditionally were the animate symbols of Nature and Spirit. As our energies connect, I am aware of the completion of a circle that is as ancient as recorded time. Now, the enchanting voice resonates within my being, and we become one.

Shakespeare's Faeries

Mystical creatures that abound and come in many forms, faeries have titillated our imaginations for generations. Faeryland, that realm one step removed from our mortal world, has provided fodder for numerous stories through the ages. This not only includes the faeries in the children's tales, such as Tinkerbell in *Peter Pan*, the dwarfs in *Sleeping Beauty*, and the Fairy Godmother in *Cinderella*, but also the faeries in the works of the premier bard himself, William Shakespeare.

In her book, *The SuperNatural in Shakespeare*, Helen Hinton Stewart says that if we considered faeries to be extraordinarily beautiful or grotesque little beings of human form, or if we think they dance on the Faery Rings and reside in the flowers and woods, as well as fly through the air on errands, either benevolent or mischievous, then we are thinking of Shakespeare creations. These are the faeries the bard made famous, or infamous, as the case may be. They play important roles in his works, including *A Midsummer Night's Dream*, *The Tempest*, and *The Merry Wives of Windsor*. In fact, almost every play Shakespeare wrote has some mention of magick. A number of them are totally devoted to the subject. In particular, *A Midsummer Night's Dream* contains one of the most creative realizations of the faery realm.

Through his plays, Shakespeare was able to preserve much of the English faery lore, such as keeping the identities of Robin Goodfellow and Puck separate from one another. The confusion often occurred because both are hobgoblins and offspring of Oberon, who is the King of the faeries.

In "A Midsummer Night's Dream," Shakespeare tells the story of Puck, who was raised by his mother with no mention of his faery origins. When he was six years old, Puck ran away from home. Alone in the woods, he fell asleep and had a dream of the faeries. When he awoke, Puck found a scroll from Oberon that gave him the magickal powers of granting wishes and shapeshifting. But Oberon placed a condition on the powers: They were only to be used to help the good and thwart the bad. If Puck followed this condition, he would be allowed into faeryland. So, Puck set out, in true hobgoblin fashion, to play out his pranks, which were usually meant to be a lesson for the mortals he engaged.

Faery Origins

The belief in the faeries continues because, for several thousands of years, plenty of people have seen them, and continue to do so. Some say the faeries are the surviving members of an ancient race of beings who have been around since 6000 B.C.E.

Because of the lack of historical documentation, the true origin of the faeries may never be known. What *is* known is that the concept of the faeries is widespread. In all parts of the world, there are stories about beings that possess supernatural or magickal abilities and take human form.

These faery tales are part of an ancient oral storytelling tradition that predates writing. Even though they have continually undergone interpretive and social transformations while being passed on for so many years, the tales remain very much the same and represent some of the earliest stories as evidenced by myth. Even in these original tales, faeries are magickal beings who both help and hinder humankind.

Each culture has it's own name for these magickal creatures who still seem to stir the embers of our imaginations. Some of these names include: elves, sprites, mermaids, trolls, and gnomes. Beautiful, ugly, helpful, benevolent, mischievous, and sometimes dangerous, faeries and magickal creatures continue to enchant us.

The modern definition of faeries describes them as mythical beings of folklore and romance with human form and magickal powers. In Middle English, "faery" refers to three things:

1. Enchantment.
2. A land where enchanted beings live.
3. The group of inhabitants of such a place.

The word "faery" is Middle French. It is derived from the Old French "fée" or "feie," which stems from the Late Latin "fata" (the goddess of fate), and from "fatum," meaning fate.

The Fates in Roman Mythology are three goddesses who determine the fate of every person. They perform their duties at each child's birth, which is when they write the destiny of the child.

In Norse Mythology, fate lays in the hands of the three sisters called the Three Norns, or The Maidens. Urd spins the thread of existence. She passes the spun thread to Verdandi, who weaves it into existence. Each day Urd and Verdandi weave the fate of the world, and by the end of the day, Skuld unravels it, tossing it back into the abyss. Similar to the Roman Fates, a Norn is present at each person's birth to declare that individual's fate.

The faery connection with fate is congruent with their spiritual Nature. It is this spiritual Nature that makes it possible for faeries to affect mortals. Faeries and mortals share a spiritual Nature, and it is this spiritual affinity that acts as the connecting thread. At times, the faery and mortal worlds come together. They meet at a kind of magickal cross-road. When this happens, it creates an energetic doorway through which mortals can enter the realm of the faery and the faeries can enter the mortal world. Most often, when the faeries enter the mortal world, they become visible.

By seeing the faeries, and by occasionally entering the energetic doorway to the realm of the faeries, mortals discovered that there was a world that exists just beyond the mortal vantage point. When the time is right, mortals, like you and me, can deliberately interact with this world and the faeries that inhabit it.

Faery Mythology, Folklore, and History

The realm of the faeries is strongly interwoven with the concept of Earth and ancestral spirits, powerful energies that permeate both the faery and mortal worlds. These energies are addressed in Celtic Mythology, specifically in the myths and legends of the Tuatha De Danann.

In the history of Ireland, five consecutive waves of invaders took control of the island. When the last wave, called the "sons of Mil," came, they drove the Tuatha De Danann, who were the people living in Ireland at the time, into the hills or "sidhe." When the people of the Tuatha De Danann went into the hills, they wove a veil of invisibility. This divided Ireland into two realms, the seen and the unseen. These hills or mounds represent another realm, a dimension of awareness that exists in a different tense, one step beyond our "ordinary" perception. It is in these hollow hills or subterranean "sidhe" mounds that the faeries still dwell.

The faeries are obviously part of a Pagan, pre-Christian religion. Within the faery lore of Scotland and Ireland are the remnants of the old religion, with gods and goddesses acting as the guardian ancestors of the clans. Every clan claims descent from a particular goddess or god. These same Pagan goddesses and gods appear in local tales, and are transformed into faery kings and queens. Living in magnificent faery palaces in the woods and by secluded streams, they act as guardians of forests, lakes, rivers, villages, and cities. In this way, the Pagan deities transformed as faeries remain a part of the land and the folk memory of the people.

Rather than being descended from the Tuatha De Danann, the leprechauns come from ancestors that are equally as old, or even more so. Accordingly, the elves and drawfs are of Norse origin, so the Tuatha De Danann proposal only accounts for certain kinds of faeries.

Some theories on the origins of the faeries suggest that elves and dwarfs are the Nature spirits and deities who were worshipped by the ancient spiritual traditions. Another suggestion is that the faeries and related magickal creatures originated from people and other beings who have died and passed on, but their collective spirit still resides in the land. This collective spirit comprises the faery.

Indeed the strength of the faeries comes directly from the power of the land, from the earth. Generations of ancestors and generations of the earth's creatures buried in the land give it a tremendous, sacred power. This sacred power is the power of the faeries.

In post-Christian times, the Pagan faeries became the fallen angels. Occasionally they were depicted as astral or Elemental spirits. With the growth of Puritanism, faeries were thought to be harmful and evil.

Whether or not they are angels or the defeated goddesses and gods of the Tuatha de Danann, the faeries are ancient spirits that are magickally tied to places on the earth. They are the sacred spirit or presence that animates and enlivens all of Nature. As the previous goddesses and gods that were the embodiment of Nature, the faeries evolved into beings who represented these magickal aspects. As mortals became more agrarian, we settled and stayed in one locale. Remaining connected and in tune with us, the faeries adapted to these changes by becoming less wild and developing more household qualities and skills.

Faeries as Friends

Faeries are found more frequently in Europe and Asia, and less often in Africa and America. They are also found in Norse, Germanic, Finnish, Lapp, and Lithuanian folklore. In terms of *Faery Magick*, the types of faeries I have included are those from Ireland; Scotland; part of England such as Wales, Cornwall, and Brittany; Germany; Scandinavia; and other European countries. Belief in these faeries in these places has been a constant for generations, and there is a larger accumulation of information about them.

Since their origin, the idea of faeries as magickal purveyors of good and bad luck, has lit many a creative fire. People want to believe in magick, primarily to spice up their lives as well as explain all those things in life that can't be explained.

Good and bad luck are often forces that you consider beyond your control. Some days you wake up and things go so right that you have to stop and pinch yourself to make sure you aren't dreaming. Other times everything goes wrong, and you wish you had stayed in bed. Faery Magick is all about being in harmony with the powers of good luck, and avoiding those of bad luck.

Faeries like befriending mortals. They enjoy doing helpful things, and as long as you keep giving them gifts in return, the magickal relationship continues unimpeded. Remember, the faeries usually believe that a gift deserves a gift in return.

In the past, the faeries controlled the crop harvest and the milk yields, therefore people would leave food and drink out for them. In return the faeries would help the crops grow, keep the milk cows productive, as well as do helpful things and bring good luck to the home and those residing in it.

House faeries like gifts of milk, sweet cakes, honey, butter, ale, and other delicacies. With the presence of ample offerings, a house faery will help with some of your unfinished jobs at night as you sleep, and bring you good luck.

In friendships between faeries and mortals, problems generally arise when the faeries feel mistreated. Most mortals who are familiar with the magickal ways of the faeries will make peace with the Nature or house faeries that live nearby.

In a metaphysical sense, this alleviates many problems, and creates a little bit more faery magick in your daily life.

There were many stories of people who have mistreated the fairies. They have been paid back by having things physically thrown about or hidden from them, catastrophic occurences, etc. Mistreating or breaking your promise to a faery is *not* something I would suggest—***ever!*** Doing so can create insufferable consequences and make you one miserable mortal.

By making friends and cooperating with the faery energy, you can make your life easier. Working with the faeries, your life becomes more aligned with the Natural forces that have been part of human life since the beginning of time. The next time you can't find your keys or your dinner burns to a crisp, remember the magickal energy of the faery: an energy that co-exists in your house with you. As an ally, it could help accomplish anything, but as an enemy, it could make your life an unending array of practical jokes—all quite educational, I'm sure. Faeries are not just mischievous, but often appear so as a means of teaching an unsuspecting mortal a lesson about life.

Time, space, energy, and form are all relative.
Appearance, reality, and identity are also relative to your
awareness.

To become more aware of the faeries and other magickal beings, it is essential that you *shift* or *alter* your awareness. It's as if you get your "mortal" out of the way for a few moments and expand your senses to include the faeries. It is much like the shift of your awareness when you are dreaming.

Because of their spiritual nature, the faeries are ever-present in your many lifetimes: present, past, and future. You are a multifaceted being who combines both physical and mental realities with spiritual realms that seem to drift just beyond our awareness. Just beyond the glimpse of an eye, faeries are the magickal forces that affect every aspect of your daily life. By better understanding and working with these energies, you can improve your chances of success no matter what you set out to do, and live happily ever after, again and again.

Modern Faery Tales

Just like in the world of William Shakespeare, faeries continue to play a part in modern storytelling. For example, in the animated film *Fern Gully* a female faery makes a mortal male tiny so he can see life from the vantage point of a faery, in the hope that he will help stop the destruction of Nature. In *Lord of the Rings*, by J. R. Tolkien, elves, dwarves, and other faery-like creatures, band together to do battle with darkness and evil.

Yoda of *Star Wars* is a modern-day version of a faery being. Like Yoda, faeries are often viewed as teachers. If you win their favor, they can teach you many things about the ways of faery magick. It is a rare honor when a magickal being comes into your life and offers to be your teacher. Make certain the faery has your best interests at heart. You can usually tell this by whether your life works better with or without the magickal help provided.

In terms of modern folklore, faeries and angels have much in common. What the angel, Clarence, does to the character George Bailey in the film *It's a Wonderful Life*, is very faery-like, particularly because George had been drinking when he had the experience on the way home from the tavern. Clarence shapeshifts George's life so that he can see what would have happened had he never been born. He creates an Otherworld reality that permanently alters how George view of his life. Magickal beings such as Clarence, who can shapeshift in space and time, are the essence of faeries.

The faery spirit, with its wry and magickal manifestations, lives within the human psyche. It is an energy that you can either choose to ignore, or to apply in positive ways. Usually, incurring the wrath of faeries involves doing something that is abusive to either the faeries or to Nature. After all, they are the stewards of Nature. As with anything, in order to work with the faeries you need to understand their decorum—what they do and don't like, as well as what offends them and what delights them.

Modern culture continues to include such magickal beings as the tooth faery, Santa's elves, and faery godmothers. Also, every Halloween, children shapeshift into little magickal beings, who go around asking for gifts of treats. If you don't respond kindly with a treat, you may wind up on the short end of some mischievous pranks, a prank similar to the type that the faeries are known to play.

Faery Magick

Faery Magick is about tapping into the powerful spiritual energy of the faeries when you make magick. This faery energy comes in many types, some kinds beneficial and others hostile. It is important to know the Natures of the different types of faeries, and to work with only those that are friendly and helpful. When working with the faeries, it can also be beneficial to know their customs and traditions.

Like so many things having to do with the faery, magick is less complicated than you think. It is not about lighting candles, burning incense, casting spells, or chanting invocations. Magick is a Natural state, a spiritual state of being, where your mind is filled with wonder. Your imagination soars and it suddenly becomes possible to follow your deepest dream. Magick can brighten everything in your life, if you just open the door to your inner spirit and let it in.

By working with the energy of the faery when you do magick, you are invoking divine beings that transcend the bounds of time. Folklore says that if you move into the world of the faeries, time moves much differently. Like Einstein's theory of relativity, the faery world and the human world are relative to one another. Because of this relativity, time moves at a different rate in the faery world, much like they say it would if you were traveling at the speed of light. Doing so can be extremely dangerous.

Because time is different in the realm of the faeries, **do not** attempt to go to the faery realm. Instead, it's much more intelligent to learn how to commune with the faeries in the mortal realm through a variety of awareness-shifting methods, many of which are described in this book.

The faery energy, as previously mentioned, is tied to Nature. This means that when you are doing faery magick, you are working with devas and Elementals that reside in a variety of Natural settings. Because of this, it is vital that you go outside into Nature when communing with the faeries. Many faeries are Nature spirits, who are often tied to the Elements of Earth, Air, Fire, and Water. There are exceptions to these ties, for example, house faeries such as brownies and hobgoblins. They are tied to homesteads, to homes, to families, to specific households, or to a specific locale.

Magick is a method where Divine and mind combine to modify reality. If everything in this world is illusion, as many philosophers suggest, then magick shifts the illusion.

Like most things in life, magickal ability is gained through practice and experience. Setting up patterns for achieving your magickal goals, and staying focused on these goals until you attain them, guarantees success in making magick.

To create a basic magickal pattern, use the three steps of *expectation, planning,* and *merging.*

✳ **Step one: Expectation.**

This is the process of determining what it is you really want. These are your deepest desires. Your expectations, coupled with your intention and desire, form the foundation of your magickal pattern. Choose things you really want, or the rest of the magickal pattern can become meaningless or even a constant irritation, such as when you find yourself somewhere you really don't want to be. In this initial step, it is important to get in touch with your needs, wants, and desires, and to determine what, in life, is more important.

One method for determining your expectations and desires is to think very generally about the things you want and don't want, such as what you like to do, where would you like to live if you could choose any place in the world, who are the people you would like around you, and what kind of life would you like to lead.

After determining your general thoughts and feelings about these questions, get more specific about what you want to do, where you want to live, and who you want in your world. Narrow it down. And then, narrow it down again. In terms of expectation, the more definitive you are, the greater the chance for the success of your magickal pattern.

✳ **Step Two: Planning.**

This is the process where you sit down and brainstorm ways of achieving your expectations. If you want a new house, then you should make a plan describing what it would take to make it happen. You have to find the house of your expectations, come up with a down payment, and get financing, so these are some of the things you might want to include in your plan. Remember, when things seem impossible magick usually kicks in, and suddenly a plan, that seemed like it would never be more than a dream, is a reality. Be prepared by planning ahead!

✦ Step Three: Merging.

This is the part of your magickal pattern where you bring in, and become one with, the energy of the faery. Merging is a process where you feel yourself become pure energy and light, at which point you connect with the eternal spirit that weaves all things together as One. This step activates your magickal pattern and makes it a reality. Sometimes the effects are seemingly miraculous.

Faery Magick is the what, when, how, and wow of ordinary and extraordinary realities blending. Being one of the oldest energies, the power of the faeries can prove to be a powerful helpmate for successful magickal patterns. You need to use this powerful energy wisely and with deliberate care. Magickal texts say that if you master faery energy, your thoughts will manifest themselves *almost instantly*. You seem to glow and your presence changes your environment and those around you. You can always tell when mortals have the favor of the faeries in their beautiful gardens, inviting homes, friendly pet companions, and their abundant resources and artistic talents.

Today, Faery Magick and faith in the faeries continues to thrive, especially with the renewed interest in Wicca, Paganism, and other Earth-spirited traditions. The faeries are still seen each and every day. As you practice the techniques I have included in this book, you, too, can tap into the spiritual power of the faeries, and commune with these magickal beings.

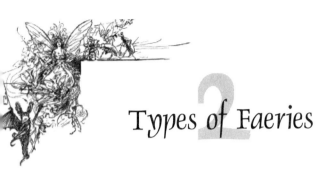

Types of Faeries

"Fairies, black, gray, green, and white,
You moonshine revelers and shades of night,
You orphan heirs of fixed destiny,
Attend your office and your quality,
Crier hobgoblin make the fairy oyes."
—William Shakespeare, *The Merry Wives of Windsor*

Journey: The Shapeshifter

I sit with my eyes wide open as the person before me shifts shape. I pinch myself to make sure I'm not dreaming. Beginning as a small, elderly looking man with elfin features, he transforms into a giant, silver-furred she-wolf. She looks in my eyes, and I can see the moon reflected in hers. The wolf beckons me to mount her back. I climb on, putting my arms around her neck. We travel so quickly that everything around us moves as if in slow motion. Images go from being blurry to suddenly very clear.

Riding along on the she-wolf's back, I see an image of a tree nymph as it scampers up the side of an ancient oak tree with a trunk the size of a small house. The oak's mighty branches reach out like giant, gnarled arms toward the sunlight. The tree nymph stops on the trunk, and looks in my eyes and, for an instant, I feel the connection between us. I am aware of the spirit of the trees, and I am the trees

and the trees are me. In that instant of complete connection, I know that life is more than the black and white
world that I thought was "real."

As I continue traveling on the she-wolf's
back, I see an image of a small winged being
who moves like a dragonfly through the woods.
She is the Element of Air, and I feel myself
becoming her and being blown about by the wind.
In this state, I realize that struggling against the
wind is futile, but to move with the wind is divine. I feel
myself blown to and fro in all directions. After a few minutes, I find myself, once again, on the wolf's back moving
through the woods.

Soon, I see an image of an enormous salamander who
looks just like a fire dragon. One of the most volatile of
Elements, Fire is the creation of life, and instantly eradi-
cates anything in its way. The enormous salamander stops
to bask in the sun, happy and content. Watching this giant
being, I know that there are two sides to everything. In
creation there is destruction, and in destruction there is
creation. They are divinely tied together.

As I continue riding, I see the image of a Water sprite
swimming in a pool. The water looks bottomless and as
infinite as all of Oneness. Time and space are relative to
experience, which is relative to the overall pattern of things.
Pools of water become creeks that become streams, that
become rivers, lakes, and oceans. And oceans become lakes,
rivers, streams, creeks, and pools of water. Each pattern in
life is part of a bigger, connected pattern that makes up the
whole of everything.

Whether Earth, Air, Fire, or Water, all life is make up
of Elements. Each Element has a lesson to teach. As embodi-
ments of Nature, faeries often directly correspond to the

Elements. These relate back to the basic beginnings of the faeries and Nature itself.

As I continue on the wolf's back, time folds into itself. She disappears and I find myself standing in front of an oak tree whose wrinkled image suggests the very fabric of time, and whose eyes look directly into mine. Its roots are like anchors that stretch deep within the earth. Its trunk, branches, and leaves move out into the air. Its entire being moves upward towards the light of the sun, signifying the Fire of life and it must have water, signifying the Water of life.

Staring into the eyes of the oak, I see a future filled with magickal beings. As both my ancestors and the entities that dwell within the land, I know the faeries are like guardian angels and spirit guides who help me along my way.

As my eyes move, I see the shapeshifter can be anyone or anything. I understand now that things are what they are on the inside, no matter what kinds of outside images they portray. Like candles, the woods, the magickal beings, and the land of illusion melts away leaving only that which remains— the eternal flame that burns in the hearts and spirits of everything that lives within the flicker of a lifetime.

Alphabetical Listing of Faeries and Related Magickal Beings

Although the concept of the faery is worldwide, the following list includes magickal beings primarily from the European cultures because they are more familiar. I'm sure there are other magickal beings that could be added, but the overall idea is to provide you with a background of the different types of faery and magickal beings, and their uses in relation to magick.

Remember that there are always differences in behavior and appearance, even within the same type of faery.

Take nothing for granted and make no presumptions when engaging the more positive types of these magickal beings. Completely avoid the negative and deadly forms of faeries.

Alvens: These are Water faeries who float around on bubbles and hate fish. During a full moon, they come on land to dance and play. They are not particularly friendly.

Amadan Dubh: This is a particularly dangerous type of faery that is greatly feared among the Gaels. They are known as the "fairy fools," and the bringers of madness and oblivion. They play faery enchantments on their reed pipes on hilly slopes and precipices after sunset.

Banshee: The name "banshee" means a woman of the faery. It corresponds to the "Fear Sidhe" or faery man. The wild banshee wanders through the woods and over the moors at dusk, and sometimes lures travelers to their death. Banshee can also travel at will to great distances. Appearing in tattered gray clothes, they are basically a sociable faeries who have become solitary through sadness and grief. They are the honorable ancestral faery women of the old clans of Ireland, who are heard, but rarely seen. They wail a blood-curdling lament just before misfortune, illness, or death occurs in their ancestral families. Their wail can kill or instantly age mortals who hear it. Banshee also avenge the death of their descendants. They generally appear either as beautiful maidens or gruesome crones. Salt water and silver can harm them.

Bendith Y Mamau: They have the ill disposition and ugly appearance of goblins, but the glamour of the faeries. Living in underground caverns, they don't care very much for mortals and they have been know to steal cattle and children, to kill farm animals, and to break important tools.

Billy Blin: A household familiar who is popularized in English and Scottish songs.

Boggart: They are known for breaking things and making trouble, but seldom do serious harm. Most old homes have a boggart. The supernatural boggart is sly, annoying, mischievous, and a prankster. They pull the covers from sleeping mortals, rap or pound on the door at odd times, or rearrange the furniture at night when you are sleeping.

Brownie: They are from 1 to 2 ft. tall and are scattered throughout the highlands and lowlands of Scotland as well as the northern counties of England. They have brown, wizened faces and hair growing all over their body, so they don't need to wear clothes (although sometimes they are seen wearing brown cloaks with hoods). As household faeries, they do unfinished jobs such as mowing, threshing, caring for the laying hens, and tending the sheep and cattle. They bring good luck to a family, providing that the family treats the brownie well. Brownies also love animals and will take care of the household pets. They adore gifts of food and drink such as milk and honey cakes, but abhor gifts and wages.

Urisks are the Scottish version of brownies.

Buccas: Residing in Cornwall, they are magickal beings that inhabit mines. Also called tinmine demons, they are the wind goblins that foretell shipwrecks.

Bwca: This is a sort of Welsh version of a brownie, but a more particular one. They can be great help around the house, but if offended they can become harmful, throwing things around the house, spoiling the milk, and ruining the beer.

Callicantzaroi: Naked, they ride about on chickens. They live in troops and are zealous in their celebrations of Yule.

Clim: A mischievous goblin that resides in chimneys and peeks out at children, scolding them when they are bad.

Clurichaun: Residing in southwest Ireland, they are renowned drunkards who both guard and raid wine cellars. The Clurichaun sing in Gaelic and have beautiful, magickal voices.

Coomlaen: These "elven steeds" appear as tall, thin, white or silvery horses who live in the forest and are always in the company of elves. As shapeshifters, the coomlaen can take the shape of their desires, but must return to the shape of a horse once during each day for at least six hours. They are fiercely devoted to one rider at a time and the bond lasts for the lifetime of the rider. The two communicate telepathically. Because the Coomlaen defends its rider, in order to befriend a coomlaen you must first befriend its rider. Coomlaens adore gifts of apples and honeysuckle. Iron is harmful to the coomlaen.

Cooshie: Also known as the "elfin hound," they live in the forest and appear as large, silver-furred wolves that move quickly with the grace of a large cat. The cooshie stay with their elfin masters, and have heightened senses, including knowing when there is any magickal, spiritual, or physical presence in their territory. Like elves and coomlaens, they have an aversion to iron. Cooshies can heal sick or injured travelers and calm troubled minds and hearts.

Corrigans: From Brittany and Cornwall, they live in the woods, near streams. Corrigans are winged faeries who like to play pranks, such as taking human babies and replacing them with changelings.

Daoine Sidhe: The immortal polytheistic group of goddesses and gods of Pagan Ireland who merged with the land, these are the cream of the crop of faeries that form a faery nation. They appear in human form, dressed in green, and are called the peaceful faeries. They preside over the faery kingdom, play sweet music, dance, ride milk-white faery horses, and are generally accompanied by their faery hounds.

Dryad: They are happy, friendly, and playful wood nymphs who live in and take care of the trees. They are born of the same seed as the place they live. Dryads are the color of tree bark or leaves and their dark green hair is extremely long and flows about them. They can disappear by stepping into a tree, as if stepping into a dimensional door. Sometimes their skin is dappled like a tree trunk. Dryads are usually very charming, sing beautifully, and particularly like willow and oak trees. Damaging a dryad's tree harms the dryad as well, but the dryad can defend its tree by creating storms and lightning.

Dwarfs: Both male and female, dwarfs are usually from 3 to 5 ft. tall, with broad shoulders, large muscles, long arms, stumpy legs, and lots of facial hair. They are quick tempered, loyal, and immune to physical damage. Working with Earth, Fire, and stone, they are found underground under mountains and hills where they mine metals and gems, especially copper. Their craftsmanship is unmatched in the mortal world. They adore gifts of both precious metals and gems.

Eash Uisge: They are the Highland water horses known for being fierce and dangerous. They have the ability to shift into the shape of young, handsome men.

Elves: According to Norse mythology, elves and dwarves are created in the time before humans from the body of Ymir, the giant. Inhabiting one of the upper worlds, and often found in Natural settings such as woodlands and forests, elves are somewhere between mortal and divine. Originally between 5 and 7 ft. tall, they were thin, strong, flexible, and quick. Their hair was usually red, blond, or light brown, and they had cat-like ears. Their cat-like eyes are green, blue, silver, or gold with slitted pupils. Through time, the elves became Elemental spirits of the land, sea, and forest, who are sometimes portrayed as small, good-natured creatures with brown skin and delicate features. Iron does not kill elves, but it can injure them. They adore gifts of quartz crystal, pearl, moonstone, and silver. In the Western world, Santa Claus and his helpers are elves.

Ferrishyn: The Manx name for the faeries, also known as the "sleigh beggey."

Fir Dearg: Also known as the "fear darrig" or the "red men," they are a mischievous, rare breed of faery, who dress in red and have red hair. Their only interest seems to revolve around playing practical jokes on humans.

Ganconer (Gean-canogh): Also known as a love faery, the ganconer is a leprechaun-type faery who appears as an incredibly handsome young male.

Called the "lover-talker," he spends most of his time seducing milkmaids and shepherdesses. Appearing in lonely valleys and fields, they are known for playing beautiful songs on their pipes, but their fate is ultimately to be alone.

Gnomes: They are elderly dwarf people who stand from 1 to 2 ft. tall, and like dwarfs, live underground except for the few times when they come up to roam in the deep forest. Male gnomes grow long beards. Gnomes live under old oak trees in heavily forested areas, and like gifts of beautiful stones.

Gray Elves: Not choosing to associate with any other magickal beings, they live in isolated meadowland. Gray elves have either silver hair and amber eyes, or pale, golden hair and violet eyes. They are very intelligent and extremely rare.

Gwartheg Y Llyn: The Welsh name for faery cattle, said to be usually milk-white in color. A farmer who gained the favor of this magickal cow was said to be richly rewarded, but the farmer who tried to lift a hand to hurt the animal would find misfortune would come to the farmer.

Gwradedd Annwn: The Welsh name for the "lake maidens," they are beautiful and desirable, but are not like sirens and nixies. They are known for marrying mortals much like the Silkee or "seal maidens."

Hobgoblins: They are the English cousins to the Scottish brownie and Welsh bwca. A house faery, a hobgoblin's favorite place is behind the kitchen fire, once known as a "hob." Once settled, they rarely leave the house, and when feeling neglected, they are known to hide keys in the most unlikely places. They are vulnerable to iron and gold. In folklore and literature, both Robin Goodfellow and Puck are hobgoblins.

Knockers: In Cornwall, they are generally helpful mine sprites that are particularly attracted to rich veins of ore. Miners of old were said to follow the sound of the knockers' tools pounding the rocks to find a strike. Knockers are also known to warn against cave-ins and floods, and as such, the miners always leave them gifts of food and drink. In Wales, knockers are known as "coblynau."

Kobold: The German name for the "little people," originally they were tree sprites who were captured and brought home in wooden boxes. The person who captured the kobold could open up the box and the kobold would do things for her or him. But if anyone else opened the box, the kobold would take revenge for being confined. They formed the basis for the original jack-in-the-box for children. They are old men the size of small children who wear pointed hoods or caps and green clothing. Loud noises and strong winds scare them. For gifts of food and milk left out at night, they will do any little job around the house and barn, such as washing the dishes, preparing meals, sweeping the floor, making the fire, or tending the farm animals. Kobolds also have the ability to cast binding spells and will go to great efforts to protect the members of the household. If mistreated, they can become truly nasty.

Leanhaun (Leanan) **Sidhe:** They are the faery mistresses or sweethearts of Scotland and Ireland. They crave love, and try to gain power over their lovers, treating them like slaves and draining all the life out of them before moving on to new lovers. Said to be an inspiration to poets and musicians, these magickal faeries act as sort of muses, giving the artist's work an otherworldly quality.

Leprechauns: They usually manage to trick their way out of surrendering their gold. Only a select few get away with a leprechaun's riches. Solitary faeries of Ireland, witty, fascinated with gold, they can pass by as a swirl of dust, knocking off your hat. They are generally 2 to 3 ft. tall, with wizened faces, bright eyes, and red noses. They dress mainly in greens and browns, and are known for their excellent shoe-making skills.

Lorilei: A solitary faery, who is beautiful and bewitching., she is known for lounging on rocky heights while singing a song of enchantment.

Lunantishee: They guard the blackthorn bushes particularly on Samhain and Beltane. If you cut a stick from the bush on either one of those days, you will suffer misfortune.

Mermaids/Merrows: They live in the airy palaces beneath the waves. They wear red-feathered caps to swim from their underwater world to ours. If a mortal steals the cap, the merrow can't get back home. The females are beautiful, the males are ugly with green faces and red pig noses. Both have fish tails and webbed fingers. Taking mortal lovers, their offspring are covered with scales.

Muryans: Cornish faeries, the word "muryan" means "ant." These are faeries the size of ants, who are shapeshifters. Every time they shift shape, they get smaller, eventually getting so small, they disappear from sight.

Nixie: They are Water sprites that inhabit lakes and seldom venture onto land. Their houses are made from seaweed and are guarded by giant fish. They are known for charm spells that convince humans to do their bidding.

Nymphs: Nature spirits who evolved into faeries, they live in clear lakes, streams, and crystalline caverns. Intelligent and beautiful, they do not like intrusion, but will be friendly if approached by a good-hearted mortal. Nymphs have the power of prophecy and take mortal lovers. They are also said to be extremely hard to avoid once they have taken an interest in you, and can occasionally be dangerous if they become obsessed with you. Often traveling in pairs, nymphs are mobile, but they can also permanently align themselves with trees, rock outcroppings, mountains, rivers, and springs. They appear as young, extremely gorgeous women, who are frequently dancers, artists, and musicians. They are amorous and have insatiable sexual appetites. According to folklore, a nymph's lifetime was the same as that of the phoenix, who outlived nine ravens, who outlived three stags, who outlived four crows, who outlived nine generations of aged mortals.

Oakman: A wood faery who lives in oak trees, the oakman is a guardian of the animals. The familiar saying "faery folks are in old oaks" speaks of their kind. The oak is considered the tree of the dead and the abode of departed spirits. Oakmen resemble drawfs with red noses, wear red toadstool caps, and have an affinity with bluebells.

Pechs (Pehts): The name used for the faeries of the Scottish Lowland, Pechs are said to be like the feens of the Highlands and the trows of Shetland.

Phouka (Pooka): Originally deadly sea horses with glossy coats and metallic-like hooves, phoukas are now often viewed as wild, mischievous creatures who are related to the leprechaun. Phoukas can employ the shape of an animal in order to play wild pranks and kill mortals. In contrast, in some stories that are told about them, phoukas that are treated kindly are known as friendly beings that help farmers.

Piskies (Pixies, Pigsies): Found frequently in Cornwall, Devon, and Somerset, England, they stand 1 ft. high (or smaller), are slim, and wear green clothes and pointed red hats. They have blond hair and green eyes, pointed ears and chins, and turned-up noses. They can also levitate and move tiny objects from one place to another. Usually friendly, they can also be mischievous, and are known to steal horses and ride them around in circles, creating Faery Rings as they do.

Portunes: These are teeny tiny faeries that are about a finger's length or less in size.

Redcaps: They live in castles and towers where evil deeds have been done so they can feed off the energy and create more of their own. They look like brownies, but wear caps made red by the blood of passing strangers at whom they have thrown stones.

Salamander: They are the powerful Spirit faeries of Fire because the salamander embodies the intuitive Element of Fire. Without the salamander, Fire would not exist. They come in all sizes and differ in appearance, but they are most often seen as being similar to a 1-ft. long lizard. They can grow larger or smaller at will.

Sometimes they are seen as a ball of gold, orange, or red light. They are very devoted and quick to defend a friend. Working with the salamander helps you develop and strengthen your intuitive side.

Seelie: A good-hearted and benevolent group of faeries who glow as they ride the winds in search of humans needing help. The court of the kindly faery host is called the "Seelie Court." "Seelie" means "blessed" in Gaelic. These benevolent faeries give gifts of bread and seed corn to the poor and provide all kinds of help to their favorite mortals.

Sheoques: Appearing human-like, they live in ancient thorn bushes and faery forts that are surrounded by ditches. Also known for their bagpipe playing, they enchant and steal children, most times returning them unharmed and happy.

Shock: They appear as a horse, donkey, large dog, or calf. They are frightening and something to get away from if, by chance, you encounter one.

Sidhe: The word means "people of the faery mounds." A distinction is often made between the "sidhe" who are seen walking on the ground after sunset, and the "Sluagh Sidhe," the faery host who travel through the air at night and are known to abduct mortals. There are also guardian "sidhe" associated with the lakes of Ireland and Scotland. These distinct categories of "sidhe" beings tie in with the testimonies of seers who divide the "sidhe" into Wood spirits, Water spirits, and Air spirits, i.e., the Elemental spirits.

Sidhe Draoi: Gaelic for "faery druids," folklore says that they took their name from the faery nymphs who taught them the magick of the trees. They are related to dryads.

Silkee: Usually found in seas and oceans, silkee first appear as seals, but become beautiful women when they shed their skin. They use their seal-skin to move from their world to this world. If their skin is taken from them, they can no longer move back and forth.

Sithich: Active Highland sprites known for being mischievous and having weapons that do their bidding, they are dexterous, child abductors, and intrude on women during childbirth. Their weapons are made of stone, shaped like a barbed arrowhead, and thrown with great force like a dart.

Sirens: They are Greek sea nymphs. The sirens' enchantingly beautiful song entices sailors, leading them to their death.

Skillywidden: Small, young faeries who cannot shift their shape or alter their size.

Sleigh Beggey: The Manx name for the faeries.

Slievegallion: Known as the "hosts," they are the spirits of mortals who have passed on into the otherworld. They fly about in great clouds, up and down the landscape. On clear, frosty nights they can be seen, and heard, fighting their battles in the air. They sometimes put mortals under their spells to help fight their battles.

Slyphs: Living for a thousand years without seeming to age, they are beautiful, changeable creatures that parallel nymphs, only they exist in the Element of Air. Living on the tops of high places such as mountains and cliffs, slyphs vary in size, are winged, transparent, elusive, and surrounded by a glowing radiance. For a very brief time, they can take on human form. They move by floating about with the wind, and as such, are known as the Spirit faeries of the Air. They inspire mortals, especially those individuals involved in the creative arts.

Spriggans: They guard the treasures of other faeries. Spriggans are ugly and dour, standing stone sprites that are said to have come over from Brittany where they are known as "korreds." Folklore suggests that they brought the original standing stones to Cornwall. They can be seen around old ruins, standing stones, barrows, giants' quoits and castles, and places where treasure is buried. They bring blight to crops, whirlwinds over crop fields, and storms. Spriggans are the ghosts of old giants, who appear small but can become gigantic at will.

Sprites: Very shy, delicate, and reclusive, sprites are winged spirits that dwell in meadows and woodland glens. There are many types of sprites, depending upon their Element. Fire sprites are very rare. As William Shakespeare describes them in *The Tempest,* "Sprites are spirits: they do not have bodies as fairies do." They adore gifts of nuts, acorns, and sweet treats, and love to be flattered by mortals.

Trolls: Originally supernatural beings in Scandinavian folklore, later they became huge ogres with great strength and little wit. Trolls are known for guarding castles and treasure, hunting in packs in the deep forest, and being deadly to mortals. They can outrun any mortal. Fire and sunlight will harm them. *Never* try to befriend one.

Trows: They are the Shetland Island version of trolls. They live in caves near the ocean or in sandy hillsides. Thought to be somewhere between dwarfs and giants, trows are dimwitted, unfriendly, and ugly. Sunlight turns them to stone or makes them explode. The Scottish Highland name for trows is Feens or Fians.

Undines: As Elemental Water spirits usually found within forest pools, waterfalls, marshlands, rivers, lakes, and riding the ocean waves, the beautiful voices of the undines can sometimes drift above the sound of the water. They inhabit underwater caves, river banks, and lake shores. They are able to influence the flow of water in streams, rivers, lakes, and oceans, as well as the plants that grow in and under the water. Undines can appear human-like and are generally shy, but friendly. Peaceful, graceful, and attractive, their skin shimmers blue-green, green, or aqua like the water. The undines are ruled by love and adore gifts of sweet-smelling perfumes.

Unseelies: They are dark, malevolent faeries, who have excessive pride, are unkind, and have malicious ways. In contrast to the seelie court, the unseelie court is one of the malevolent faeries, who are hostile and harmful. *Stay away* from them and *do not* engage them in any way.

Water Sprites: They are closer to the traditional concept of a mermaid, and are the marine counterparts of leprechauns.

Wight: A supernatural being or creature that is very hardy. Every tree has a wight who is its guardian. An old Scottish verse says,

"If you call me blessed wight,
I'll be your friend both day and night."

Magickal Times
for Faery Magick

Journey: Magickal Faery Gathering

I had a dream last night, a dream that seemed very real, both when I was dreaming and when I awoke in the morning.

The dream begins with me walking along a winding dirt road. The road is very worn and its boundaries are carefully outlined with large granite and crystal stones. At times I feel I know where I'm going along this road, and other times I feel I'm lost. At times, familiar signs here and there assure me that I know where I'm going, and other times, the signs are completely unfamiliar, and once again, I feel totally lost.

Wandering and wondering around within the space between here and there, and now and then, I happen upon a magickal being dressed in a soft blue tunic, who seems especially intent on where she is going. Her elfin features *are small and delicate, her hair light and long, and her eyes are a golden green color and slitted like a cat's. She is tall and thin. I beckon the elfin lady to stop a moment, and I ask her, "Where are you off to in such a hurry?"*

Drawing her attention to me unfortunately also draws the attention of her companion, a silver-furred wolf-like creature that immediately comes at me, snarling and barring its teeth. I step back slowly, and she calls the creature back with a brief hand signal. She looks at me with her golden eyes for a moment before speaking. "I'm on my way to the celebration of the faeries," she says.

With my curiosity aroused, I ask her if I might accompany her. She nods and I step in line with her, and we continue down the road. Her wolf-like companion stays at her side, barely tolerating me, while constantly sniffing and looking at our surroundings. The wolf hesitates now and again, but continues by his mistress's side.

A little further down the earthen road we encounter another magickal being. He is covered with thick brown hair. His face is dark brown, and shriveled with the lines of time. Each movement he makes seems to course another highway of wrinkles across his face, signaling where he's been in life. The old, wizened being stumbles and falls. I offer him my hand, and he lifts himself back to the road, and thanks me. As his hand touches mine, I feel a well of energy that stretches out past generations. I glimpse a knowledge that electrifies my very core and, at the same time, I feel a complete and absolute peacefulness fill me. From the two polarities, I realize that the distance from one point in infinity to the next, from here to there, from now to then, is both an instant and eternity, depending upon my perspective and in what realm my awareness dwells.

We all travel together further down the rock-lined, earthen road. Soon we encounter magickal beings of all shapes and sizes. Like ourselves, all of them are going to the magickal faery gathering. The closer we get to our destination, the more I feel the magickal energy of the faery filling the well of my soul with their ancient spiritual knowledge, wisdom that has been passed down even before the beginning of time.

I stop on the edge of the road for a moment to look at a giant sunflower in full bloom. Its golden petals stretch out to their fullest. A sweet scent catches the attention of my nose, and looking down I see the source is a mass of white honeysuckle blossoms that cover the ground just below the sunflower.

Bending down to better smell the sweet aroma of the flowers, my eyes move down the vine-like stalks of the honeysuckle, resting on the image of a small, bluish-green winged creature sitting on a leaf just below one of the fragrant blossoms. I smile, and the tiny faery sprite smiles back. For a moment I feel a connection with both the faery and the essence of honeysuckle. My being is suddenly fragrant and my inner beauty blossoms in that magickal moment.

The elfin lady, clad in the blue tunic, beckons me to her side, and once again I am moving along the path towards the faery celebration. I see a fabulously lush garden filled with flowers of every kind. The garden and its flowers grow in a circular formation around a giant rock altar, and there is a narrow earthen path that outlines both the garden and flowers within it. The giant rock altar looms up out of the North point of the circular garden.

I feel myself swept up with the others as we all form a circle around the magickal garden, placing our feet on the narrow path and joining hands. On one side of me is an oakman with his red toadstool cap and red nose, and on the other side is a dwarf, a large rotund individual, who seems jovial and a little gruff all at the same time.

With joined hands, we form a giant ring around the garden. We dance clockwise around the garden, again and again, careful to stay within the narrow path to avoid treading on the breathtaking flowers blooming all around us. With our intention combined, we send a cone of white light that moves out across the land until it completely covers the entire planet, our solar system, and then the universe. As we send out the white light, we know that our Earth is sacred. She is our Mother in a very real way. As the light fills the land, I can feel the magick everywhere, in everything and everyone. For that moment and always, I am filled with the magick of the faeries, with the magick of each moment, with the magick of the universe...

Faery Magick Timing

Many a faery tale begins with the words, "Once upon a time, though it was not in my time, or in anybody else's time." Customarily in the world of the faery, time seems to stand still and last forever. This is akin to the concept of the "eternal now" in magickal traditions. The experience of "now" can last forever if you learn to slip into that fold of time and space that is boundless and goes on forever, like a movie being played over and over. As modern physics has determined, time is relative to where you are and where you are going. This is particularly true in faeryland where time and space shift into the Otherworld of timelessness.

Because faery magick is about combining the timeless power and spiritual energy of the faery with traditional techniques of magick, part of what you need to know is exactly when and where in the "eternal now" the faeries are most prevalent. Knowing this makes connecting with these energies easier. By adding faery energy to your magick, you can create stronger and more powerful magick.

There are specific times of the year and day when the energies of the faeries are at their peak. When you do magick at these times, you are invoking the full power of the faeries. Because the mortal and faery worlds are distinct and separate, timing becomes an important element. There are certain times that the two worlds come together naturally. These are not the only times you can do faery magick, but they are the times more conducive to contact with the realm of the faery. Again, these are times when the veil between the worlds is most thin, and thus the points when they come together as one.

In magick, timing is everything. It's easier to flow with the natural timing of things than to try to force energy to move in directions that it doesn't naturally flow into. It's obvious that if you continually try to swim upstream, the current will eventually wear you out.

Understanding the influences that are happening at a given time not only adds energy to your magick, but also makes it so you don't find yourself struggling against the overall flow of things.

This is why knowing and using astrology is especially helpful for those who practice magick. I suggest that you become familiar with and use an ephemeris every day. Have your natal chart done either by a reputable astrologer or over the Internet, or use astrology software.

Get to know the aspects in your chart. From there, become familiar with the basic aspects of the planets, the Sun, Moon, and how they interact. As you do this, you will also get to know when the most conducive times are during the day, week, month, and year, to do magick.

Sabbat and Esbat Faery Portals

The eight Sabbats (quarter and cross-quarter days) and Esbats (full moons) during the year are the key times when the portals open and the mortal and faery worlds connect. At these times, those from both worlds can more readily interact with either. By virtue, these are the best times for doing Faery Magick because they are the times when the faery energy is most present and accessible.

The veil between the mortal and faery worlds is at its thinnest during *portal times*. Keep in mind, the veil is more metaphorical than physical. After all, there is no veil or separation, except in your awareness. You perceive a veil or separation mainly because your awareness is present in the mortal world here and now, rather than in the faery world there and then. Keep in mind, you are always just one step away (in awareness) from the faery world. The steps are just easier to make on certain days and nights, such as the Sabbats and Esbats.

Many a faery tale begins with a traveler walking on a path or lonely road on the night of a full moon. On his or her way, the traveler always meets a faery or magickal being. You, too, can take advantage of the faery power of the full moon. Every year usually has 12 full moons, but on some years there are 13. The full moon represents a time of optimum energy and magickal power. Because of the heightened lunar activity and increased light at night, many of Nature's creatures, including the faeries, are out and doing things.

The Sabbats are the other times that are most identified with faeries. Most of us are familiar with Shakespeare's depiction of faeries romping through the woods in his play *A Midsummer Night's Dream*. Wisely, he chose the best faery timing possible for the setting of his play–the Sabbat night is most commonly associated with the faeries. Like Shakespeare, you can tap into your natural skills and wisely chose the optimum days and eves for doing Faery Magick. The following Sabbat listing can help you to do just that:

⚹ Imbolc, Bridget's Day

Also called the Feast of Pan, this Sabbat is at the beginning of February, when Nature first starts coming to life, and the ewes (sheep) get their first milk of the new season. It also marks the beginning of agricultural season, and as such, is the time of the first plowing. A traditional ritual was one where children went house to house with a plow asking for treats on this day. A house that gave no treats was likely to find its front yard haphazardly plowed up. This little ritual is particularly reminiscent of a faery prank. Also, because Bridget is considered to have woven the first cloth in Ireland, a cloak known as "Bridget's Cloak" is left outside the front door on this eve, and by morning, it is believed to acquire magickal healing powers. This Sabbat is a good time of year for clarifying your magickal expectations and goals.

⚹ Spring Equinox, Ostara

The Spring or Vernal Equinox is on or about March 21st. It marks the beginning of Spring when Nature grows stronger and more vital. Traditionally associated with Ostara, the Easter bunny is a faery-like being who symbolizes the fertility of Spring both in the form of a rabbit, an animal that propagates easily, and the egg, the symbol of new life. In folklore, the rabbit is the one who knows the formula for making a potion for immortality. It is a time for appreciating and honoring Mother Nature, her creatures, and the faeries. Traditionally, on the morning of the Spring Equinox, wash in water scented with crushed flowers to bring you love, luck, and good health. This is an excellent time of year for planting the seeds of new magickal goals.

⚹ Beltane, May Day

This Sabbat is at the beginning of May. On May Day, long poles are decorated with flowers, ribbons, and colored eggshells, and people dance around them, singing songs and celebrating the sunshine and sexual power of Spring. The two greatest festivals on the leprechaun's calendar are May Eve (on the first of May), which begins the warm half of the year, and Samhain, which begins the cool half of the year. Irish legends tell of competitions between the faeries on the eve of May Day. Every seven years, the competitions are more intense. It is also on this eve that the faeries mix barley with the dew gathered on a mountain top at midnight to make a strong brew. With one drink of the brew, the faeries dance for hours on end. Food and drink are traditionally left out at night to ward off faery mischief.

Midsummer's Eve, Summer Solstice

An eve sacred to lovers, Midsummer's Eve is on or about June 21. It marks the height of the growing season when all of Nature is in full swing. It is a time of optimum growth and absolute florescence. Midsummer's Eve at dusk, especially if the moon is full, is considered the best time for viewing and experiencing the faeries. Because of this, it is also one of the best times for doing successful Faery Magick. All Natural waters have healing powers on this eve, and you can bathe in the ocean, lake, river, or stream to help heal any illness.

Lughnassad

This Sabbat is at the beginning of August. It is the celebration of Nature when everything is growing strong and maturing, a time of fruition. Coming toward the end of summer, this day marks the beginning of the harvest festivals. It's a time for climbing the hilltops and gathering berries and early fruits of the season. Celebrate and honor the faeries and be sure to give them gifts of a few of your finest harvest foods. Use the power of this day to move your magickal pattern forward to fruition.

Harvest Festival, Autumnal Equinox

The Fall or Autumnal Equinox is on or about September 21st. It is the time to reap what you have sown throughout the year. As the traditional day of giving thanks for the harvest, you should leave out offerings of food and drink to the faeries, especially butter and milk. Also, they appreciate gifts of flower garlands, special dances, and beautiful songs on this eve. This is a good eve for asking the faeries for protection, family harmony, and good fortune. Remember, the relationship with the faeries is always one where they do something for you, and you, in turn, do something for them. The balance of give and take is standard fare, especially when exchanging gifts with the faeries.

⁎ Samhain, Halloween

This holiday comes at the beginning of November when the veil between this world and the faery world is at its thinnest, thus making it easier for contact with the faeries and working with them when doing magick. Faery lore states that if you want to see them, you should visit their hill on the eve of Samhain, and walk around the mound nine times counterclockwise. This will open a door into the hill. Through the door you can see the faeries all dancing together and playing sweet music.

⁎ Winter Solstice, Yule

The Winter Solstice on or about December 21, is a faery-like and magickal holiday. In Western culture, Santa Claus, that jolly old elf, is very faery-like with his sleigh filled with gifts and his magickal reindeer that fly through the sky. Santa's helpers are all elves and Santa's parents were of the faery. Ginger cookies and milk are a favorite of the faeries, especially the gnomes on the eve before Yule. This Sabbat marks the beginning of the Cycle of Life and offers a time for reflection on the past and present, and into the future.

Other significant times of the year for doing faery magick include March 15th, the Ides of March, which is the time of the festival for river nymphs and water faeries; August 7th, the Lammas Tide, which is the time when the faery hills and dwellings become illuminated as they socialize with one another; September 29th and November 8th, Gwynn ap Nudd, which is the time when the lord of the faeries opens the doors that stand between this world and the faery realm; and November 11, Lunantishees, which is considered a good night to stay indoors. It is also the faery festival of the spirits that guard blackthorn trees, a favorite of faeries.

Times During the Day

Just as the Sabbats and Esbats act as faery portals, there are specific times of the day when faeries are more accessible. Within shadow and light exist an interplay that bleeds over into every aspect of life. In the movie *Ladyhawk*, the evil wizard makes it so that during the day the man appeared as himself, but the lady appeared as a bird, and at night the lady was herself, and the man was a wolf. In "real" time, their human images never met except at those brief moments when it was neither dark nor light–at dawn and dusk. These are also the times you can most easily see and communicate with the faeries.

Just before and just as the early morning light dawns, before the rays of sunlight break through the prevailing darkness, the energy of the faery is especially strong and ever-present. If you venture out at this time of morning, or at dusk just as the Sun sets, your chances of encountering faery energy is much greater because these are the times when the mortal and faery worlds have more of a proximity. Most faery activity ends before midnight.

The faery world is one step away from human reality, and often you only catch glimpses of these magickal beings out of the corner of your eye. When you do catch them in your sight, if you blink, doubt what you are seeing, hesitate in your thoughts, or look away for any reason, these magickal beings vanish.

The faeries make themselves known in many subtle, not always visible, ways. For example, animals will often sense the presence of a magickal being by staring fixedly at a particular spot. Animal companions such as cats, dogs, and birds are particularly adept at this.

Faery Magick Locations

Because the faeries were originally Nature spirits, the places where they are most likely to be found are forests, meadowlands, near streams and brooks, glens, hilltops, caves, and other natural settings. Different types of faeries can be found in particular places in Nature because of their fondness for a particular type of Element. For example, undines, merrows, and Water sprites can be found in creeks, waterfalls, fountains, and ponds, whereas dryads, gnomes, and sidhe draoi are more likely to be in places like forests, groves, glens, and heavily wooded areas. Keep in mind that every type of faery and magickal being is different. Their habits, likes, and dislikes, provide clues as to where you can find them.

Whether searching for a particular type of faery or just wanting to experience faery energy in general, it is important to get outdoors. It is there that the spirit of the faery resides. From the immense strength and endurance of a giant oak or cedar tree to the bright, delicate blooms of wild poppies and fragrant roses, the world of Nature is alive with the beauty of the faery. One of the main prerequisites for doing Faery Magick is to get out into Nature, no matter whether it's a secluded retreat, a national forest, your backyard, or balcony or roof garden. The further out in Nature you get, the more the chance of encountering faeries. Even so, every Nature setting, no matter how small, with plants, flowers, trees, animals, birds, bees, butterflies, and other insects, has the spirit of the faeries in it. Their energy dwells there and can be used in Faery Magick.

If you're searching for a particular type of faery, then begin by studying its characteristics and lore, including where it lives. Go to these kinds of locations, and see if you can find traces of faery energy. Do this at least seven times before trying another faery location. Seventh time's a charm when working with the faeries.

When faeries and other magickal beings are near, you may feel as though someone is watching you. Then when you look around, you find that no one is there. You may have the feeling that something is touching you, such as a soft butterfly's wing, but when you look, there is nothing there. You may smell a wonderfully fragrant aroma that seems to come from nowhere, or you may suddenly hear whispers, breathing, or hushed giggling. You may see objects glowing in the distance. Also, as you become more sensitive to how it feels, it will be easier for you to identify when faery energy is present.

Natural occurrences, such as four-leaf clovers and Faery Rings, have long been associated with the spirit of the faeries. The rarity of a four-leaf clover makes it a magickal find. Children seem to find lucky clovers with ease. Folklore holds that when you find a four-leaf clover, you will be incredibly lucky, clairvoyant, and suddenly able to see the faeries. To do so, it's important to carry the four-leaf clover with you at all times.

Faery Rings

Another gateway into the faery world is the Faery Ring, usually consisting of mushrooms, grasses, or rocks in a circle a Faery Ring can also be a Natural, circular-shaped meadow surrounded by blackberry or other bushes, or even a small hilltop with grasses growing in a circular pattern. These are places where the faery celebrate and dance, often in circles holding hands, when no one is around. One story says that the hobgoblins create the circles when they steal the horses and ride them around and around until a magick Circle is created.

Whether or not created by dancing faeries or hobgoblins, a Faery Ring is one of the ideal places to observe the faeries and other magickal beings. *Do not* step into the Circle. If a mortal steps into their Circle, he or she may wind up dancing merrily with the faeries. What seems like only minutes may indeed become three to seven years, or more.

If you get trapped in a Faery Ring, a friend can help get you out of it by reaching in and pulling you out *without* stepping into the circle. It's best never to step inside the Faery Ring. Instead, position yourself outside of the Ring where you can see it easily, but in a safe and protected place, such as behind a group of trees, bushes, rock outcroppings, or behind a small hill.

Faery Rings are also among the favorite meeting places of leprechauns. If you put one foot or hand, in the Ring while they are invisibly gathered there, you will be able to see them clearly. If you put both feet or both hands in the Ring, you may become their prisoner and have to obey their every command. Unless you have somehow offended them, you will probably come out of the experience unharmed. They will have a laugh at your expense, a pastime the leprechauns, as well as faeries, find especially amusing.

Although they often enjoy themselves at the expense of mortals, faeries usually do it in the spirit of fun and, often, there's a teaching intention as well. Always remember to respect the ways of the faeries, and in turn, they will help you rather than hinder you. When you remain authentic and respectful when dealing with all faeries and magickal beings, your magick will be more powerful, and you will have more fun and fewer problems.

Creating A Faery Ring

To attract faeries and other magickal beings to your door, you can create your own version of a Faery Ring by drawing a circle in the dirt where you want your Ring to be. The circle can be as big (a large meadow) or small (a flowerpot) as you want or have space for, depending on your needs and living environment.

After you have drawn out the Ring, gather together enough stones to line the parameter of your magickal Faery Ring. One by one, set the stones on the outline of the Ring so they all touch together. Take your time when doing this, fitting the stones together while thinking about the ring you are creating and its purpose.

Once you are done outlining the circular ring with stones, sit or stand back for a few minutes. Now in your mind's eye, imagine a thread of bright white light energetically connecting the stones together. Imagine light weaving the stones together in a clockwise motion, around and around the circle at least seven times.

As a finishing touch, plant flowers and herbs that attract the faeries in and around the Ring. Select your favorites and the faeries will be pleased. Faeries and other helpful magickal beings are attracted to all beautiful things connected with the living spirit of Nature.

Optimally, your Faery Ring should reflect the passing of the seasons. For example, plant some narcissus, which bloom in early spring, and perhaps some daffodils, tulips, irises, all of which bloom shortly thereafter. Add a few daisies or annuals, and a rose bush or three or seven (miniature roses are great in Faery Ring flower pots). These plants keep on blooming until autumn, and in some milder climates, they bloom continuously. Be sure to snip all spent blooms back, and water the plants regularly.

Creating a Faery Ring is one of the simple and enjoyable ways in which you can get in touch with Nature, and in turn, the magickal energy of the faery. The next section further explores the ways in which you can work with Nature to bring the energy of the faeries into your life in order to do magick. Being magickal themselves, they bring a potent power into your overall life patterns and your personal goals, which define who and what you are and what you like, dislike, dream about, value, do, and accomplish.

Getting In Touch With Nature

You can create places in your immediate environment that are more conducive to faery energy. By growing magickal gardens, you not only create a place for the faery to come but also a place that you have a personal connection with. When you garden, part of your energy becomes imbedded in the soil, seeds, and plants you tend. The soil, seeds, and plants also become part of you through your skin, and, when you eat the fruits, vegetables, nuts, and herbs that you grow. There is a constant exchange of energy.

A magickal garden is a place where you can connect with Nature, and as such, draw in the energy of the faery. Plant flowers and plants that express who you are. Roses are fragrant, gladiolus are showy and elegant, and candytuft have delicate, snowy flowers that eventually spread everywhere. No matter how large or small your garden is, the most important thing is that it is a place you want to be, a place where you and the faery can communicate.

If you're trying to attract certain types of faeries, then you might want to set up certain conditions in your garden, such as a waterscape, wooded area, or place where there is lots of flowers. The idea in faery magick is to make it all work towards the object of your desires. With intention, you can make your dreams come true in ways traditionally reserved for faery tales. Faery tales *can* come true. They have been around, in one form or another, for thousands of years. These stories are all glowing examples of the enduring quality of the faeries and other magickal beings.

The Golden Rules of the Otherworld

The Otherworld of the faery is traditionally located in the mounds, known as the "sidhe." Each mound is connected to the other mounds by energetic faery paths known as *trods*. The Celts were careful not to build on the trods because they believed it would bring bad luck. When the Irish say "in the way," it alludes to something obstructing a trod or violating some place that is part of the sidhe. There are plenty of accounts that describe houses or barns that were built on the trod that either burned or suffered other misfortunes. These accounts support the notion that they are harmful energy fields. These harmful fields or lines of energy are the opposite polarity of the powerful ley lines that crisscross the countryside. As such, they are harmful to people and to animals, suggesting they can be used as a protective field to keep mortals away from the faeries and their dwelling places.

The Otherworld is always here or there, depending upon where your awareness is at the moment. Needless to say, most mortals are not normally aware of the Otherworld of the faeries. What usually happens is you get glimpses, oftentimes out of the corner of your eye. As you become more adept, you can learn to see the faery world for longer periods of time at will, and eventually to be both "here" and "there" in the Otherworld simultaneously, through a process known as *doubling out*. This also forms the basis for *remote viewing*.

If you happen to find yourself in the Otherworld of the faeries, never eat or drink anything–**NEVER!** Doing so often causes you to remain trapped in the Otherworld. Remember that what seems like very little time in the faery world can be a long time in the mortal world. This is also true when you are in a merged state while meditating, praying, or doing magick; time almost seems to stand still.

It may become a problem if you spend too much time in faeryland. When you come back, you find that things have changed because so much time has passed.

The golden rule of the Otherworld is: *If you are given a faery gift, you need to repay it.* In turn, if you give a gift to the faery, one will be given back to you. You must always be respectful of the faery energy, including your actions toward plants and animals.

Many faeries and magickal beings have become disillusioned with humans' treatment of Nature. It is because of this that they stay away from people, and if contacted, they can be hostile. Like some animals, they have learned to fear and be wary of the human attitude toward Nature. They have plenty of reasons to feel and act in this way.

Humans use chainsaws to cut through trees without thinking of the life they are ending. The chainsaw may be mightier than the tree in a physical sense, but it is ultimately the tree deciding whether people continue to live on this planet. Trees breathe in carbon dioxide and convert it to oxygen, and humans breathe in oxygen and convert it to carbon dioxide. If we keep cutting trees down at the present day rate, eventually the balance between oxygen and carbon dioxide will be so off-kilter and the air quality so poor, we will most likely cause the extinction of the human species, not to mention just about everything else living on the planet Earth.

With faeries that are beneficial and helpful to humans, it is important to stay in their good graces. I strongly suggest leaving offerings, especially of food and drink. Make offerings to the faeries by going out and planting something in Nature or giving an animal companion affection. These are things the faery consider good and repay in kindness.

Always remember that the faeries can be a source of unlimited luck or limitless frustration. By observing the golden rules of the Otherworld, you can avoid offending them. Begin today to make offerings to the faery to get in their good graces and stay there. At the same time, by working with Nature, by nurturing animals, and by planting seeds, flowers, trees, and bushes, you help heal and strengthen the Earth, not to mention beautify your immediate environment.

The Elements and Four Directions

Many times, you are naturally drawn to one Element or another. For example, you can't keep some people out of the water. They are always swimming, boating, or bathing. Some people are so in tune with the Earth that they have the proverbial "green thumb," such as the group of individuals that created the Findhorn Garden with the help of the plant devas and spirits.

At the core of our physical reality, everything is energy, energy that is moving and interacting with other energy. Energy moves in certain patterns like waves and fields, and these patterns are influenced by the elements as they interact with one anther. Harmony is the blending of different Elements while at the same time decreasing their conflict. This Elemental harmony is an essential part of your Faery Magick because all of the faeries and magickal beings are keyed into either one or more Elemental energies.

North/Earth:

> This represents the original faeries that came from the Earth including dwarfs, gnomes, and the sidhe. Spiritually, it is the grounding of your life, and metaphysically has to do with your ability to be pretty much stable and solid in your being.

East/Air:

> This represents the faeries that are connected to Air, such as the nymph-like sylphs or the sprites who resemble dragonflies and butterflies. Spiritually, it is the breath of your life, and metaphysically has to do with your ability to become the wind and connect with the "Divine voice."

South/Fire:

> This represents the faeries that enjoy Fire and light, such as salamanders. Spiritually, it is the creative Fire of your life, and metaphysically has to do with your ambition and drive to get what you truly desire.

West/Water:

> This represents the faeries that reside in the Water, such as nymphs and undines. Spiritually, it is the Water of your life, and metaphysically has to do with emotional flow and feelings as well as your ability to flow with life.

The Magickal Ways of the Faery

"When I touch that flower, I am touching infinity. It existed long before there were human beings on this earth and will continue to exist for millions of years to come. Through the flower, I talk to the Infinite, which is only a silent force. This is not a physical contact. It is not the earthquake, wind, or fire. It is the invisible world. It is that small voice that calls up the fairies."
—George Washington Carver

Journey: Entering Faeryland

From my garden, I walk down the earthen path toward a magnificent ash tree. Its many branches stretch out like arms, in the chill of the late afternoon sun. As I move closer, I see that the base of the tree is about 30 ft. around. I walk past a bed of lavender and the sweet fragrance fills my senses, sending me back in time to when I was a young girl playing in my Nana's garden. I take another deep breath and continue on.

The brittle leaves covering the ground beneath the ash crunch and crackle as I walk under the canopy of the massive tree. I sit down between two gnarled roots, sinuously growing out from the base of the tree. Nestled against the trunk, I watch the shadows of the branches and leaves dance upon the ground. Like the ever-changing ash tree, the shadows have no permanent pattern. The shadows dance over my skin and I merge with them. The play of shadows shows me the essence of the ash. Supple strands of light and darkness weave in the wings of the wind, their canorous voices merging into one.

Immersed in the whispering shadows, my eyes travel from the ash to the ground. I focus on my surroundings and notice a large circle of wild mushrooms in the grass directly to the left of the massive tree. Within the circle, a clump of brightly colored marigolds grow. Their orange and gold heads bob slightly, to and fro, in the gentle wind. I think, "How strange. This is the wrong time of year for marigolds to be blooming."

I gasp as the earth within the mushroom circle suddenly begins to crack and spread apart. The yawning chasm in the ground continues to expand and break away until the entire circle is a deep hole. Recovering from my initial surprise and fright, I stand with my hand resting against the ash tree and I crane my head to look down the gaping crack.

I hesitate and move closer, more out of curiosity than caution. As I look down the opening, I see a path descending into the depths, leading to a land beyond.

As if being guided by an unseen hand, I enter the hole. Instead of being surrounded by darkness as I first expected, the underground cave is illuminated with a crepuscular light whose source emanates somewhere behind the distant shadows that stand before me. For the first 90 feet, two sheer granite walls stretch out on either side of the narrow earthen path. Soon the walls give way to a grassy meadow covered with wildflowers of every color. As I move closer to the source of light, I see that the tall, distant shadows are actually two giant oaks, standing side by side, about 9 feet apart. They form the gate to the enchanting land of the faeries.

I glide through the oak gate and a blinding golden light forces me to shade my eyes as I look around at dozens of exquisite earthen houses crowned with thatched roofs. My eyes adjust to the light, and I notice the finely crafted houses dotting the perimeter of a bright golden circle in the center of town. The circle is covered with golden bricks that appear to be the source of the brilliant streaming light.

I notice a procession of small people riding white ponies approaching. The people wear green, hooded cloaks and their diminutive features are soft and pleasing to the eye. The braided manes of the small horses hang with tiny silver bells that tinkle as the procession moves closer. In front rides a young woman with luminous skin, emerald green eyes, and long, flowing golden hair. Behind the young woman rides a green-haired, golden-eyed man playing a small harp. The melody from the delicate faery harp, intermingled with the tinkling silver bells, creates an enchanting symphony of sound.

The young woman smiles as they ride by and the young man nods his head as his nimble fingers continue to stroke the strings of the sweet singing harp.

I follow the procession through the village. Everywhere around me the faery folk celebrate, dancing, arms linked, singing ancient songs. Their beautiful voices join together in a perfect cadence.

I watch the singing and dancing for a long time, but eventually close my eyes and drift to sleep. When I wake up, I find myself, once again, under the massive ash tree where my adventure began. I look at the Faery Ring in the grass. To my amazement there are now twice as many marigolds blooming as there were before. I touch the blossoms gently for a few minutes, smiling and remembering the enchanting land of the faeries. As the afternoon light dims and the air grows colder, I stand up, stretch my body, and follow the earthen path back to my garden.

Faery Offerings

Because the faery energy originated in the spirits of the old agricultural goddesses and gods of the Earth, they controlled the ripening of the crops and the milk yields, and thus offerings were given to the faeries at regular intervals. This includes the Sabbats, Esbats, and other faery times. The faeries represent Natural powers that can either make your life flow or make your life a total struggle. Giving offerings to the faeries is a way of helping the energy in your life flow and come together.

Helpful faeries are generally vegetarian (they don't eat the flesh of animals), and traditionally like sweets, fruits, cakes, brews, and other gifts from the Earth. One of the ways to ensure faery goodwill is to leave the first and last fruit of any harvest out for the faeries. In addition, it is a good idea to leave a small portion of any of your Sabbat feasts for the faeries. In Cornwall, the custom is never to scold a child who has spilled milk, because the spilled milk is perceived to be a gift to the faeries, and scolding would make it appear to be given grudgingly.

In England, people traditionally left offerings of sweet milk and bread on their stoves for hobgoblins and other house faeries to encourage the presence and protection of these magickal beings. Other foods that the faeries are fond of include ground ginger, barley, sugar candies, butter, milk, and honey. If you like, you can put your faery offerings on your pentacle platter or in a consecrated basket that you can put in your garden or backyard. Also, compost is a form of faery offering in that the food is given back to the Earth (home of the faeries) in order to enrich the soil so that more things can grow. Following is a list of Faery Magick food and brew offerings:

Beer

This is made from fermented barley, a favorite grain of the faeries. Beer-making is a process that requires the blessings of the faeries, particularly if you want everything to come out tasting "good." In exchange, the faeries are fond of offerings of beer, especially barleywines, bocks, and Belgian ales.

Cakes and Candies

Like children, the faeries have a sweet tooth that is satiated by cakes and candies.

Dairy Products

Because of their association with farm animals and the first milking at Imbolc, faeries appreciate offerings of milk, butter, cheeses, and so forth. Because milk is associated with the Mother, it is a favorite of faeries. If milk either goes bad or is spilled, it is seen as an offering to the faeries.

Fruit

Traditionally, the first and last piece of fruit on a fruit tree is left as an offering to the faery energy. The faeries are fond of all kinds of fruit is left, such as apples, peaches, apricots, nectarines, plums, and pears.

Honey

The faeries' sweet tooth is satisfied by a bit of honey. Offering wild honey is best.

Juice

The faeries have a fondness for fruit juices, which were traditionally termed "the nectar of the gods." They prefer naturally sweet juices, such as apple, grape, and cherry.

Spices

The faeries are attracted to spices that are aromatic, such as ginger, bay, thyme, rosemary, cinnamon, and basil.

Teas

Faeries are fond of teas, especially those made from sassafras, chamomile, and vanilla. Various teas have a soothing and healing effect on them.

Vegetables

As with fruits, oftentimes the first and last part of a harvest, such as the last corn stalk, is left as an offering to the faeries. Besides corn, other vegetables that the faeries especially enjoy include carrots, summer squash, beans, tomatoes, and sugar peas. When chopping vegetables, take the last piece and put it in the compost as an offering to the faeries.

Water

Being one the basic Elements, faeries prefer water that is pure and natural, with no chemicals. Mountain streams, with water that's as pure as the Earth itself, are what the faeries like best.

Wines and Spirits

Certain house faeries were usually given the task of protecting the cellar, the storehouse of beers, wines, and spirits. Wine-making, like beer-making, is a process the faeries can help or hinder. The faeries are always appreciative of an offering of wine and spirits to enjoy in their celebrations.

Faery Magick Color Correspondence

Different colors evoke different emotions and moods. Because of this, colors can be used as powerful focals in Faery Magick. Almost everyone has a favorite color, and what better way to "show your true colors" than to empower your magick making with the divine colors of flowers. The beauty of flowers in your garden, home, and workplace naturally uplifts you and those around you.

Both cultivated and wildflowers appeal to faeries, as do flowers that might be considered garden weeds. What's important when employing flower power is to focus on working with living flowers whenever possible–making the connection is much easier. When you use cut flowers in your spellcrafting, make every effort to select *freshly* cut ones. Refer to the following color correspondence list for more information on the magickal qualities of color and corresponding faery flowers:

White

Magickal Qualities: Positive communication with the faeries, divine inspiration, guidance, and protection, uniting power, motivation, purity, illumination, lunar power, innocence, love, peace, oneness.

Faery Flowers: Alyssum, aster, baby's breath, candytuff, daisy, gladiolus, hollyhock, jasmine, lily, pansy, peony, petunia, primrose, rose, snapdragon, tulip, stock, zinnia, hyacinth, narcissus, crocus, orchid, rockcress, masterwort, bachelor's buttons, sweet woodruff, camellia, sweet marjoram, chamomile, caraway, anise.

Purple/Violet

Magickal Qualities: Faery Magick communication (especially with faery nobility such as faery queens and kings), second sight, higher wisdom, spiritual healing, heightened awareness, psychic powers, ancestral lore, sacredness, protection, Faery Dream Magic.

Faery Flowers: Petunia, tulip, verbena, coneflower, pansy, violet, lilac, lavender, wisteria, anemone, iris, crocus, monkshood, chive, bellflower, fushia, hyacinth, hydrangea, blazing star, purple sage.

Blue

Magickal Qualities: Faery Magic healing, loyalty, divination, psychic power, learning from the faeries, higher wisdom, purification, protection from harmful faeries, flexibility, introspection, sensitivity, flow, harmony.

Faery Flowers: Aster, bellflower, columbine, delphinium, forget-me-not, grape hyacinth, lupine, morning glory, primrose, bachelor's button, gentian, crocus, lily of the Nile, bluestar.

Pink/Rose

Magickal Qualities: Faery Magick love, romance, friendship, family, balancing emotions, kinship, kindness, compassion, charm, glamour, enlightenment (rose pink).

Faery Flowers: Rose, petunia, stargazer lily, tulip, hollyhock, balloon flower, begonia, clematis, cornflower, foxglove, geranium, aster, carnation, impatiens, gladiolus, sweet pea, tulip, Cerise Queen yarrow, azalea, anemone, dahlia, dianthus, hydrangea, camellia, purple basil. (Use caution when ingesting roses, as some are **poisonous**.)

Green

Magickal Qualities: Healing, growth, abundance, good luck, shapeshifting, fertility, money, creativity, birth, healing, ambition, prosperity, regeneration, renewal, Nature.

Faery Flowers: Lady's mantle (with soft green-yellow heads), angelica, artemisia, flowering kale, hosta, shellflower.

Gold/Yellow

Magickal Qualities: Faery Magick communication, understanding, teaching, learning, intelligence, mental agility, comprehension, creativity, solar power, wealth, expanded cognition, attraction, imagination.

Faery Flowers: Calendula, chrysanthemum, cosmos, daisy, gerbera daisy, daffodil, tulip, snapdragon, sunflower, yarrow, marigold, lily, arnica, feathered-amaranth, wallflower, core-opsis, dahlia, leopard's bane, Mexican tarragon, goldenrod.

Orange

Magickal Qualities: Faery Magick happiness, fair play, justice, healing, meditation, joy, generosity, success, friendship, productive action.

Faery Flowers: Lily, marigold, chrysanthemum, poppy, butterfly weed, canna, feathered-amaranth, fuchsia, gazania, gerbera daisy, black-eyed Susan, Mexican sunflower, tulip.

Red

Magickal Qualities: Faery Magick love, romance, passion, sexuality, creativity, vitality, action, courage, focus, enthusiasm, power, animation.

Faery Flowers: Rose, verbena, dianthus, petunia, canna lily, gladiolus, nasturtium, Oriental poppy, petunia, snapdragon, stock, tulip, dahlia, zinnia, columbine, blanket flower, scarlet sage, pansy.

Faery Magick Flowers and Herbs

All of Nature, in its wild and splendid beauty, is home to the faeries. They frequent fields of wildflowers, grassy meadows, and wooded forests, as well as gardens, fountains, and lakes. If you plant, and lovingly care for, the flowers, herbs, bushes, and trees in your garden, the faeries will most certainly come. The easiest and most practical way to do this is to plant a flower and herb garden.

Garden faeries have a fondness for thyme, clover, and foxglove. To attract faeries to your garden, plant pansies, snapdragons, foxglove, roses, sunflowers, honeysuckle, yarrow, lilac bushes, and petunias, as well as verbena, daisies, cosmos, rosemary, thyme, and lavender. Always leave at least a small section of the garden *uncultivated* and wild to pleases the faeries.

Also keep the powerful healing qualities of flowers in mind when using them in magick-making. Bach Flower Remedies, for example, are potent flower healing formulas you can use at home. They were formulated by Dr. Edward Bach in the 1930s, and remain popular today. There are also certified Bach Flower Remedy practitioners. Bach Flower Remedies have been successfully used to treat negative states of mind, and "Rescue Remedy" has become a staple in many people's medicine chests. The mother tinctures for the Bach Flower Remedies are still made from Dr. Bach's original flower garden. Refer to the following alphabetical listing for more helpful information on the magickal qualities of flowers and herbs.

Barley

Add to magickal brews and potion, for protection, healing, and empowerment. Scatter it around an area such as your garden or other sacred space to rid the area of unwanted energies.

Basil

Awakening your second sight, instilling passion, and good luck, as well as attracting prosperity, strengthening love spells, and bringing happiness into your home.

Blackberry

Protection, healing, and to attract wealth, and an offering to the faeries. They enjoy the berries, jam, and the wine.

Blessed Thistle

Expands your awareness, repels negative energies and harmful faeries, and empowers Faery Magick spells.

Bluebells

Making and wearing a crown of bluebells on your head on Beltane Eve will help you see the faeries. A ring of bluebells is a favorite gathering spot for garden faeries.

Catnip

You can always find faeries, and your feline friends, at the catnip patch in your garden. Plant some catnip to entice a faery pet companion. Catnip encourages feelings of peace, love, playfulness, and happiness. During a full moon, combine catnip with chamomile and mint to make a faery dream tea, and drink it before you go to sleep to dream of the faeries.

Carnation

Carnations draw healing and helpful faeries to your garden, especially winged ones. Plant carnations next to your house, for example, in a flowerpot next to your front door, to protect, bless, and bring good health to you and your family.

Chamomile

Chamomile attracts money and love, and is used for purification, meditation, and protecting the home from harmful energies. Plant chamomile as a garden ground cover to entice tiny flower faeries. When walked on, it smells delicious! Sprinkle the flowers around your home to get rid of unwanted energies, or drink chamomile tea before you go to sleep to dream of the faery.

Clover

Faeries traditionally love clover. Two-leaf clover can be used in Faery Magick spells to attract a lover; three-leaf clover dispels negativity brings protection; four-leaf clover brings money, good luck, and prophecy (plus you can make an ointment with it to help see faeries). When you are in the woods or the garden and you find a four-leaf clover, hold it in your hand, and then carefully put seven grains of wheat or barley on the clover. Grasp the clover and grains in your hand to see the faeries. Finding five-leaf clover represents treasure, but only if you give it to someone you care about.

Cowslips

To discourage unwanted visitors and to attract wanted ones, plant cowslips in front of your house or grow them in flowerpots tied with colorful ribbons on your balcony. A favorite flower of the faeries (also known as the faery cup), cowslips are under the faeries' care and protection. A ring of cowslips indicates a doorway to faeryland and may point the way to faery treasure.

Daisy

On Beltane Eve, make daisy chains and wear them around your neck to see the faeries. Use them to decorate your altar, and scatter them around the edge of your magick Circle to invite the faeries in. Plant plenty of hardy daisies, such as Shasta and English daisies, in your garden and around the yard to encourage frequent faery visits.

Dandelion

Dandelion wine is a favorite of faeries. Drink dandelion tea to heighten your psychic abilities. Pick a dandelion puff ball on the night of a full moon, call in the winged faeries of the Air, make a wish, and then blow the puff ball. As it floats away, your wish will float to you.

Foxglove

A beautiful, favorite flower of the faeries, its florets are reportedly worn by faeries as hats and gloves. Also called faery's petticoats, faery's thimbles, faery's cup, and folk's glove, as its petals are used as a source of clothing for faeries. Plant foxglove near your front door to attract helpful faeries. Tie three sprigs of foxglove together with a white ribbon and put it under your bed to encourage divine dreams of the faeries.

Heather

Associated with faery queens and otherworldly adventure, a Faery Magick love flower that instills passion, expands awareness, and makes the ideal offering on Beltane Eve to the faeries.

Hollyhock

Use hollyhock to attract wealth, abundance, success, and for healing. The white and pink blossoms are particular favorites of the faeries. The tiny leaves that shoot up at the base of the blossoming plant are incredibly potent in magick-making. Plant several hollyhocks around your home to bring material gain and prosperity to your family. As a healing herb, gather hollyhock blossoms when they are freshly bloomed and eat them to promote good health. They are deliciously tender and taste like mild green onions.

Honeysuckle

The sweet scent of this sacred flower uplifts your senses and promotes second sight and otherworldly adventures. To see the faeries, make honeysuckle crowns during a full moon and wear them on your head with the flowers touching your forehead. Plant plenty of honeysuckle around your garden, for example, letting it weave up a trellis. Honeysuckle attracts honeybees, helpful faeries, and wealth.

Irises

A flower of wisdom and faith as well as eternal beauty, plant irises in your garden to attract noble and helpful faeries, especially faery queens and kings.

Jasmine

Jasmine is used in love spells to attract sacred and spiritual love. Dream pillows stuffed with jasmine encourage dreams of the faeries and faeryland. Use it in sachets and love charms to attract love and prosperity.

Lavender

Snip off a lavender flower and stem, roll the flower in your fingers, and then hold it up and inhale its scent. Do this for several minutes before doing Faery Magick spells to expand your awareness and promote a harmonious state of mind. An herb of love, purification, and protection, tie colorful ribbons around the sprigs of a lavender bush in your garden or in a flower pot to attract helpful faeries. Use lavender oil for anointing and in ritual baths, and use the flowers in sachets and charms.

Lilac

The fragrant scent of lilac brings helpful flower faeries into your garden. Use lilac in magick spells for protection, to strengthen memory, and to encourage a sense of peace and harmony.

Marigolds

A favorite of the faeries, use marigolds for protection and to strengthen psychic abilities, such as second sight. Create a ring of marigolds in your garden to sit in and meditate, or put a flowerpot of living marigolds next to your bed to encourage dreams of faeryland.

Marjoram

A Faery Magick love herb that can be used for fertility and marriage magick, especially love potions. When grown in your garden, it invites joyful and happy faeries.

Meadowsweet

A sacred herb of the faeries, used for love spells, to warm the heart, and to promote passion, peace, and joy.

Milkweed

Faeries and butterflies, especially monarchs, like milkweed, so plant plenty of it in your garden. Add milkweed tassels to dream pillows to encourage dreams of faeryland. When milkweed pods open up in autumn, use them for wish magick on a windy day by catching the blowing seeds, making a wish, and then releasing the seeds again into the wind.

Mint

Use mint in a dream pillow to dream about winged Air faeries. Sprinkle mint, marjoram, and rosemary around your home to protect it and rid the area of unwanted energies. Drink mint tea to expand your awareness, increase your focus, and strengthen your concentration.

Mistletoe

An herb of the in-between times of dawn and dusk, and a favorite of Fire faeries. Faeries hold mistletoe in their hands or carry it to keep themselves eternally beautiful and youthful. Gather mistletoe on the sixth night of the moon or on Midsummer's Eve. Use the wood to make a powerful protection and healing talisman, amulet, or wand. Because it grows every which way (upside down, upright, and sideways), it's the ideal herb to add when doing spells that push the proverbial envelope. A sacred herb of the goddess of love, it is especially useful in love spells and for getting rid of unwanted energies. Hang three sprigs of mistletoe in your bedroom to bring faery dreams of prophecy. (Note: **Never** ingest the berries of the mistletoe, as they are **poisonous**.)

Mugwort

Use this herb for protection from harmful faeries, to promote prophetic dreams. Wear a crown of mugwort on Midsummer's Eve to communicate with the faeries. Mugwort tea can be used to wash Faery Magick crystals and gemstones. (***Do not*** drink the tea.)

Pansy

A favorite flower of Oberon, king of the faeries. Used in Faery Magick love spells.

Passion Flower

Sprinkle the flowers on your doorstep and in your home to bring peace and harmony and to attract protective and happy faeries. Tie small bundles of passion flowers together with colorful pink and red ribbons and put them in your bedroom to attract your beloved.

Peony

Used for protection and to attract helpful faeries, plant peonies close to your home.

Rose

The apple of the flower kingdom and a faery favorite, plant roses in your garden and dedicate them to the flower faeries to assure that helpful faeries visit often. Use roses in

Faery Magick love spells, for healing, to bring good luck, and to attract wealth and abundance. Sprinkle rose petals on the ground on a full moon and dance upon them or take a rosebud bath to see the faeries, or drink rosebud tea to dream of faeryland. (Remember to use caution when ingesting roses, as some are **poisonous**.)

Rosemary

Also called elfleaf, plant rosemary in your garden to keep unwanted faeries away and encourage helpful elves. Used in love spells, for purification, to uplift moods, and to strengthen mental focus. Take a rosemary bath to expand your awareness.

Saffron

A Fire- and winged-faery favorite, use saffron to strengthen spells, especially healing and love spells. Also used for seeing into faeryland.

Sage

An herb of protection, purification, longevity, prosperity, and mental focus. Carry sage to increase your memory and expand your awareness. Burn sage and cedar to rid an area of unwanted energies. Tie several sprigs of sage together with a white ribbon and put it under your bed to ward away nightmares.

St. John's Wort

Called the "leaf of the blessed," this herb protects you from harmful faeries and can be used in healing spells. When picking, first ask permission from the faeries and then use your left hand to pluck the herb.

Sunflowers

A favorite flower of the faeries, make sunflower crowns and wear them during a full moon to encourage visions of faery queens and kings. Use the seeds in prosperity, fertility, and love spells.

Thyme

Excellent for attracting helpful garden faeries, sprinkle thyme around your sacred space, home, doorstep, and windowsills, to invite the faeries into your home. Take a thyme bath to expand your awareness and to see faeries, and carry thyme when you are walking in the woods. Any place that wild thyme grows is a spot sacred to the faery. As a healing herb, thyme is a natural antiseptic.

Vervain

Called the "Enchanter's Herb," use vervain in love spells, for protection, and for prophetic dreams of the faeries. Sprinkle it on the altar or around your magick Circle to purify your sacred space.

Violets

Plant violets around your home to protect it and to invite helpful faeries into your yard and garden. Make and wear violet crowns on a full moon to see the faery queens and kings. This is a powerful love flower used in love spells when mixed with others such as rose, yarrow, lavender, and daisies.

Faery Magick Trees

To the faeries, trees are alive, sacred, and divine. All trees have a spirit. When you cut a tree, you kill the spirit within it. The dryads or tree wights are probably the most familiar of these spirits. Trees also represent the *three worlds*—of subterranean (roots), middle earth (trunk), and celestial (branches and leaves)—and thus serve as a Natural bridge between worlds.

There are many ways to access the magickal powers of trees. You can sit under a tree and meditate, carefully climb a tree, sleep beneath a tree or in a tree house, as well as use pieces of the tree's wood and leaves in magick-making. Take a cue from Julia Butterfly Hill (*www.circleoflifefoundation.org*), the author of *Legacy of Luna* (Harper SanFrancisco), and find time to really communicate with the spirit within a tree. Julia spent more than two years living in a 1,000-year-old redwood, named Luna, in Humboldt County, California. Her heroic actions were intended to stop Pacific Lumber (a division of Maxxam Corporation) from butchering Luna and the ancient redwood forest in which she resided. Named one of America's Most Admired Women by *Good Housekeeping* magazine, Julia braved storms, helicopters, and bozos. She helped to remind us all of the sacred and magickal nature of trees and the forest in which they grow.

You, too, can tap into the magickal qualities of trees when doing Faery Magick. By spending time with trees in Nature you can access their powers of and communicate with tree dryads and wights. For example, sit or lay under the apple tree for an hour or so in your backyard, walk in the woods, or picnic under a large oak in the park. I also invite you to try some of the Faery Magick tree spells in this book. Refer to the following alphabetical list for some of the key magickal qualities of trees:

Alder

Key magickal uses: Protection, divination, a bridge to faeryland

Almond

Key magickal uses: Wealth, success, love, to expand your awareness.

Apple

Key magickal uses: Love, immortality, fertility, happiness, attracting helpful faeries.

Apricot

Key magickal uses: Love, creativity, mental clarity, expanded awareness.

Ash

Key magickal uses: Communication, knowledge, healing, magickal agility, sacred union, creative expression, rebirth, prophecy, justice, the World Tree.

Bay Laurel

Key magickal uses: Divination, bridge to faeryland, prophetic dreams, purification, protection, expanded awareness.

Beech

Key magickal uses: Fate, ancestry, inheritance, second sight.

Birch

Key magickal uses: Rebirth, structure, protection, formation, regeneration, pre-germination, a new start and beginning.

Cedar

Key magickal uses: Purification, protection, prosperity, healing, wisdom.

Cherry

Key magickal uses: Love, joy, playfulness, divination.

Dogwood

Key magickal uses: Protection, enchantment (four-petal flowers attract helpful Earth, Air, Fire, and Water faeries).

Elder

Key magickal uses: Protection, blessing, abundance, creativity, strengthening spellwork.

Elm

Key magickal uses: Insight, spiritual progress, healing, birth.

Hawthorn

Key magickal uses: Ancestry, shapeshifting, prosperity, family, inheritance, sacred union, Love Magick, fertility spells.

Hazel

Key magickal uses: Clear sight, mystic wisdom, healing, purification, meditation, divination, dowsing.

Hazel

Key magickal uses: Fertility spells, knowledge, protection.

Holly

Key magical uses: Divinity, concentration, organization, intelligence, ancestory, sacred union, victory, promise and renewal of hope, rebirth.

Oak

Key magickal uses: Endurance, ancestry, love, fertility, vision, protection, regeneration, justice, faith, loyalty, victory, success, a doorway to faeryland; the dwelling place of faeries.

Orange

Key magickal uses: Love, prosperity, divination, good luck, joy, happiness.

Peach

Key magickal uses: Friendship, love, good luck, passion, playfulness, joy.

Pear

Key magickal uses: Union, joy, happiness, prosperity, completion.

Pine

Key magickal uses: Protection, purification, regeneration, love, prosperity, abundance.

Reed

Key magickal uses: Healing, expanded awareness, magickal agility.

Rowan

Key magickal uses: Protection, healing, attracting helpful faeries.

Spruce

Key magickal uses: Enlightenment, awakening intuition, a sense of well-being.

White Poplar (Aspen)

Key magickal uses: Rebirth, ancestry, harmony, peace, preventing illness,.

Willow

Key magickal uses: Faery visions, birth, healing, fertility, enchantment, shapeshifting, attracting Water faeries.

Yew

Key magical uses: Rebirth, adaptability, flexibility, strength, ancestry, transformation, protection, regeneration, dreaming, longevity, divinity.

Faery Magick Animals and Insects

Both wild and domesticated animals are connected with the faeries. Faeries especially love small dogs and ponies. Examples of faery watchdogs are *petitcrieu,* a tiny and beautifully colored faery dog from Avalon who wore a sweet-sounding bell around his neck; and the *cu sith,* a watchdog of the Scottish Highlands. Faery horses can be fierce and have the power to shapeshift, with the most well-known being the horses of the Tuatha De Danann.

Other domesticated faery animals are white, brown, or speckled faery cattle, such as the *dun cow* and the *elf-bull.* Faery cows and bulls are said to make the herd flourish. Another pet companion that is most often associated with faeries is the cat.

Wild birds, such as the eagle, owl, and wren, hane been connected with faeries throughout folklore. There are folktales about the Selkies and Roane, the seal people, as well as some larger-than-life beavers. Salmon and insects were also considered faery creatures. To blend a little "animal magnetism" into your Faery Magick, refer to the following alphabetical list of animals and insects for their magickal qualities:

Ant

Learning to be here (now) in the moment, developing patience, humility, working in your community, planning, goal-setting, and attracting Earth faeries.

Bee

Accomplishing tasks, following through, working in harmony with nature, communication with others, messenger of the faeries, reincarnation, attracting winged faeries, cooperative ventures, and world peace.

Blackbird

Developing your magical abilities, wisdom, prophetic dreams of the faeries, ancestry, using camouflage for protection, and flexibility.

Bluebird

Happiness, mirth, mental agility, joy, positive thoughts, modesty, faery messages, and divine inspiration.

Bluejay

Faery mischief, playfulness, boldness, cunning, controversy, spotting trouble and potential problems, communication, agility, and adaptability.

Bull

Fertility, personal power, shapeshifting, magickal strength, attaining goals, breaking down barriers, pushing the envelope, and courage. Faery bulls make herds flourish.

Butterfly

Transformation, metamorphosis, transmigration, shapeshifting, rebirth, embracing your visions and dreams, moving to new places, and represent and help with winged faery messages and visits.

Cardinal (Redbird)

Positive parenting power, courtship, attraction, increasing personal charm, improving musical abilities, and developing your creative talents.

Cat

Poise, agility, cleverness, cunning, stealth, secrets, vigilance, persistence, transformation, shapeshifting, developing psychic abilities, and the ideal Faery Magick companion.

Cow

Appreciation of others, creating harmony, healing, honor, prosperity, sustenance, and endurance.

Crane

Longevity, reincarnation, transmigration, shapeshifting, ancestral contact and communication, and increasing dancing or running ability.

Cricket

Good luck, healing, harmony, working in unison with Nature, developing your voice and singing talents, and magickal timing.

Cuckoo

Developing musical talents, beginning new ventures, divine inspiration, playfulness, faery mirth and mimicry, and improving your performance and entertaining abilities.

Deer

Developing compassion, kindness, gentleness, proceeding with caution, learning tenderness, learning to be watchful, secrets, attunement with Nature. The stag's magickal qualities are ancestry, lineage, strength, courage, Faery Love Magick, and honor.

Dragonfly

Shifting awareness, expanding perception, lucid dreaming, transmigration, developing magickal abilities, and winged faery messages, greetings, and guidance.

Eagle

Faery inspiration, courage, wisdom, creative power, faery messages and gifts, intense magickal power, expanding your imagination, seeing the larger picture, and developing keen powers of observation.

Falcon

Swiftness, intense magickal power, insight, developing psychic abilities, answering questions, faery gifts and guidance, expanded awareness, and shapeshifting.

Finch

Love, passion, joy, new beginnings and adventures, successful choices and decisions, enthusiasm, attracting winged faeries, and animated energy.

Firefly (Lightning Bug)

Enlightenment, illumination, personal florescence, building enthusiasm, developing skills in the creative and performing arts, surprises, and attracting winged faeries.

Fox

Magickal Qualities: Camouflage, developing your powers of observation, secrets, cunning, persistence, endurance, and speed.

Frog

Letting go of old patterns, developing new abilities, releasing grief, getting rid of bad habits, predicting the weather and bringing rain, attracting Water faeries, new beginnings, and renewal.

Goose

Ancestry, wisdom, abundance, prosperity, and protection of home and material possessions.

Hare (Rabbit)

Faery Fertility Magick, love, rebirth, good luck, abundance, speed, keeping secrets, creative power, living by your wits, and agility.

Hawk

Divination, foretelling, seeing the larger picture, stamina, endurance, and expanding awareness.

Hen

Attaining personal goals, prosperity, building community, new beginnings, and discerning the pecking order.

Horse

Faery Magick companion, divine inspiration, expanding awareness, quickness, shapeshifting, stamina, and learning how to use power correctly.

Hound/Dog

Developing loyalty (both to yourself and others), Faery Magick companion, protection of home and family, friendship, companionship, heightened senses, tracking ability, intuition, developing instinctual awareness, integrity, and loyalty. Faeries especially love little dogs such as beagles and poodles.

Hummingbird

Joy, romance, love, divine messages, winged faery visits and gifts, healing, and opening yourself up to the Earthly delights and pleasures.

Ladybug

Faery gifts, joy, happiness, Natural balance, enlightenment, and rebirth.

Lizard

Lucid dreaming, healing, shapeshifting, mystery, regeneration, visions, expanding awareness, and courage. The salamander teaches how to use passion for creativity, developing personal energy, igniting ideas, and discovering hidden talents.

Moth

Shapeshifting, Moon Magick, expanding awareness, Faery Dream Magick, developing psychic abilities, and winged faery messages and visits.

Mouse

Successfully dealing with small details, scrutiny, invisibility, developing focus, and doing one thing at a time.

Owl

Learning discernment, knowing the difference between truth and deception, transformation, trusting your first impressions, secrets, developing your intuitive skills, and Moon Magick.

Praying Mantis

Protection, heightened awareness, survival, endurance, prayer power, magickal timing, and faery messages.

Robin

Parenting power, stewardship, sharing, protecting home, family and pet companions, and improving singing abilities.

Raven

Developing intuition, Moon Magick, divination, expanded awareness, Air faery visits and messages, and magickal power.

Salmon

Regeneration, prophecy, divination, Water faery wisdom, and dreams of faeryland.

Seal

Developing intuition, trusting your hunches and gut reactions, shapeshifting, charm, glamoury, ancestry, and attracting Water faeries.

Seagull

Moving beyond your imagination, going with the flow, opportunities, divine faery messages, attracting Air and Water faeries.

Sheep

Fertility, new beginnings, maintaining balance, gaining confidence, prosperity, and abundance.

Spider

Fertility, new beginnings, maintaining balance, creating your personal web of life, developing your Faery Magick dreaming skills.

Swan

Grace, flow, eloquence, divination, faery dreams, transformation, awakening magickal power, attracting Water and Air faeries.

Unicorn

Beauty, love, friendship, learning the gentle side of life, developing magickal and psychic abilities, occult wisdom, and dreams of faeryland.

Wolf

Developing your senses, loyalty to family, steadfastness, prophetic dreams, new ways of doing things, endurance, the art of invisibility, and cunning.

Wren

Quickness, divination, faery messages, and Faery Dream Magick.

Faery Magick Stones and Metals

Silver, gold, copper, lead-free pewter, crystals, and gemstones are all used in Faery Magick. Iron and steel are *not* used. The traditional faery stone is quartz crystal or a stone with quartz veins within it. Other favorite faery stones of Earth faeries, such as the gnomes and drawfs, are rose quartz, amethyst, amber (a tree resin), staurolite, and emerald.

To see the faeries, focus your intention on encountering faeries while holding a quartz crystal that is milky and filled with faery frost as you meditate or sit quietly in Nature. While sitting in Nature, try singing (if you are of good voice) to quickly bring the faeries to you. I had the good fortune to find a faery frost quartz crystal under a giant oak tree in the woods near my home. It has quickly become my most powerful Faery Magick stone.

Crystals and gemstones can also be used as Natural power boosters in Faery Magick as well as doorways to the Otherworld of Faeryland. Both crystals and the human body contain silicon.

This forms the very real physical basis for our connection with quartz.

You can apply the energies of stones in Faery Magick to amplify healing and protective powers and for stimulating psychic abilities such as second sight and astral travel. Refer to the following list of stones for more information on stones and metals and their magickal uses:

Amber

Actually a tree resin, used for Love Magick, happiness, divination, protection, attracting dryads and other Earth and Air faeries such as the drawfs.

Amethyst

Protection, healing, love, divination, dreams of faeryland, banishing nightmares, mental clarity.

Aquamarine

Attracting fresh and sea Water faeries, mental clarity, gaining positive flow, Water Faery Magick, inspiration.

Aventurine (green)

Magickal Qualities: Adventure, faery dreams, imagination, healing.

Bloodstone

Creativity, vitality, circulation of energy, higher knowledge, healing, ancestry, business negotiation.

Carnelian

Personal power, sexuality, creativity, past lives, protection, courage, focus, motivation, attracts Fire and garden faeries.

Citrine

Mental quickness, Faery Dream Magick, dispels negativity, insight, empowerment, shapeshifting, attracts Fire and Earth faeries.

Clear Quartz

A favorite faery stone, used for healing, divination, meditation, shapeshifting, seeing faeries, developing second sight and psychic abilities, purification, protection, and balancing energy.

Diamond

Strength; healing; empowerment; faery inspiration; protection; memory; prosperity; endurance; clarity; truth; attracts large, colorful winged faeries, faery queens and kings, as well as drawfs and gnomes.

Emerald

Faery Love Magick, healing, patience, growth, meditation; attracts garden and woodland faeries and faery queens and kings.

Flint

Protection from enemies; harmful faeries can be warded away with flint and iron.

Fluorite

Faery Dream Magick, developing psychic abilities, harmony, peace.

Garnet

Friendship, faithfulness, strength, protection, virility, trust, balance.

Jade

Faery Love Magick, protection, wealth, purification, meditation, harmony, dispelling negativity; attracts helpful woodland and garden faeries.

Lapis Lazuli

Psychic development, divination, shapeshifting, empowerment, moving energy, knowledge, wealth, creativity, protection; attracts faery queens and kings.

Malachite

Shapeshifting, willpower, communication with the faeries, peaceful sleep, visions, healing, prosperity.

Milky Quartz

This faery frost stone can be used for meditation and all kinds of Faery Magick. Those found in Nature have the strongest magickal power.

Moonstone

Moon Magick, good fortune, fertility, Faery Love Magick, healing, receptivity, intuition, divination, artistic pursuits, balancing emotions.

Rose Quartz

Friendship, Faery Love and Healing Magick, romance, balancing emotions, faery inspiration and gifts, adapting to change, forgiveness, attunement, faith, fertility, compassion.

Ruby

Strength, magickal faery power, protection, insight, creativity, passion, friendship, clarity, attracts faery queens and kings.

Sapphire

Psychic development, creativity, passion, stimulates energy centers, communication with the faeries.

Staurolite (Fairy Cross)

Faery stone of connecting with Nature, faery gifts and messages, divination, second sight, prosperity.

Topaz

Faery messages, knowledge, loyalty, higher love, creativity.

Faery Magick Altar and Tools

The altar is a sacred table and represents a meeting place between the mortal and divine worlds. A table, fireplace mantle, bureau top, sideboard, or steamer trunk, can serve as your indoor altar. A large flat stone, tree stump, garden bench, patio table, or other sturdy surface can be used as an outdoor altar.

Put the candles, incense, stones, flowers, and your Faery Magick tools on the altar just prior to doing spells, rituals, and other magickal works. I like to match certain decorative items of the altar to the seasons. For example, put daffodils and tulips on the altar in Spring, roses in Summer, crimson and golden leaves and corn sheaves in Autumn, and pinecones, mistletoe, and evergreen garlands in the Winter.

You will find that when you approach and stand before your altar with its burning incense, lit candles, and tools, you are immediately enveloped in an atmosphere of mystery and magick. This helps move you into an "altared" state of consciousness, which is particularly conducive for magick. Traditionally, the altar is taken down once you are done with your magickal work, but some individuals leave their altars up all the time.

Position your altar in the North, East, or center area of your sacred space, depending upon your preference. Try a couple of positions, and then select the one that works the best for you. My Faery Magick altar is in the North because the North direction represents ancestral wisdom.

Once you have selected the location for your altar, cover its surface with an altar cloth to protect it when you are doing magick. Natural fabrics, such as cotton, silk, linen, and wool, make the best altar cloths. The cloth can be any color. I also like to change the color of altar cloths to match the seasons. You don't necessarily need to use a cloth when you are working outdoors, for example on a flat rock or tree stump.

Generally, the altar top can be divided in half, the left side being the feminine Goddess side, and the right side being the masculine God side. You can place statues or representative images of the faeries, the Goddess, and God, on your altar as well as your Faery Magick tools. Keep the feminine and masculine polarities of the altar in mind when putting items on your altar. For example, put your athame and sword on the right side of the altar, and your cup and cauldron on the left.

To begin making Faery Magick, you will need a wand, an athame, a cup, and a pentacle. You can paint or cut runes, your initials, the tool's name, oghams, and other magickal symbols on your tools. Take time to carefully think about the decoration you would like before permanently marking the tool, and make certain that the decoration matches the tool's intended use. As you continue in your practice, you can add more tools to your altar. For further information, refer to the following listing of Faery Magick tools:

Athame

Associated with masculine Fire, the athame is a knife without iron or steel that is used to cut the magick Circle. I suggest that you dull your athame's edges for magickal use to avoid accidents. *(Remember to keep all knives in a safe place, away from children.)*

Bell

Associated with Air, the silver bell is usually rung at the beginning and ending of Faery Magick and to call in the faery guardians. Use the silver bell to summon faeries, as a fertility charm, and for protection from harmful energies.

Broom/Besom

The besom (pronounced *beh-sum*) is used for protection and purification purposes. A simple Faery Magick broom can be made from straw or grass tied around a leafy branch of pine or oak. The broom can also be used for astral travel to faeryland.

Cauldron

Associated with Water, the womb, and the Cauldron of Regeneration, this is a three-legged pot with an opening smaller than its base, traditionally used for cooking potions and brews. Filled with water or oil, it can be used for scrying.

Cup

A feminine symbol of Water, the cup or chalice holds water, juice, or wine on the altar. It is usually made of stone, clay, copper, lead-free pewter, silver, and is often stemmed rather than with a handle.

Cord

Symbolic of the cord of life, and used to mark the Faery Ring, it is 9 feet long and usually white, green, or brown.

Drum

A bridge to faeryland, the drum (traditionally called a Bodhram) is associated with the elements of Air and Earth. Drumming puts you in an altered state of consciousness that is conducive to making magick.

Faery Magick Journal/Book of Shadows

This is a journal containing rituals, potions, spells, as well as Faery Magick encounters, and your magickal impressions and ideas.

Incense and Censor

Associated with Fire and Air, burn incense to attract helpful divine energies. Say your prayers and wishes directly into incense smoke. If you are sensitive to smoke, try scented oils and an aromatherapy diffuser, or put a few drops of scented oil in a small pan of boiling water to disperse the fragrance.

Pentacle

This is a five-pointed star surrounded by a circle that represents the Elements of Earth, Air, Fire, Water, and Spirit. The pentacle is a powerful protection and meditation tool. It is also used as a pentacle platter (usually wooden) to hold cakes and faery offerings.

Robe/Cloak

Your robe or cloak is your Faery Magick skin. It can be made of any fabric or color, and any design. Whenever you put on your robe, you know you are ready for magick-making. Men can wear tunics and trousers instead of robes.

Sword

A small sword of bronze, not iron or steel, can be used to focus magick power, enhance your psychic abilities, to tap into ancestral wisdom, and to protect you from harmful forces.

Wand

Also called the Silver Branch, the faery wand is a rod of power and acts as an extension of your arm and hand. Made of wood (usually oak or apple) about the length of your forearm, the wand is the most ancient of tools. It is used to walk between worlds (the mortal and divine), for healing, meditation, astral travel to faeryland, and to direct magickal energies. (Refer to Chapter 6 for complete instructions for making your own wand.)

Consecrating Your Faery Magick Tools

To consecrate means to make sacred and divine. By consecrating your tools, you imbue them with divine blessings and power. Consecrate your Faery Magick tools outdoors (if possible) at dawn, noon, twilight, or midnight. I have found that dawn and twilight work best for this purpose because these are the times when I usually encounter faeries.

Before consecrating your tools, smudge them with cedar and sage smudge to get rid of any unwanted energies. Then, consecrate each tool individually by blessing it with the Elements of Earth (soil), Air (incense), Fire (flame), Water (water), and Spirit (scented oil) in that order. Put the Elements on the tool. For example, rub clean soil on your cup, pass it through the incense smoke, the flame of the candle (swiftly), dip it in or sprinkle it with water, and then rub it three times with scented oil. As you apply each Elemental representation, say:

> *"With this Element,*
> *I consecrate this tool to the helpful faeries.*
> *So be it! Blessed be!"*

Next, present the tool to the directions of North, East, South, West, and center, in that order. Now face the altar, and say:

"I charge this tool by the Ancient Ones,
By the divine powers and blessings of the helpful faeries,
By the powers of the sun, moon, planets, and stars,
By the powers of Earth, Air, Fire, Water, and Spirit
I consecrate this magickal tool.
May it serve me well.
So be it! Blessed be!"

Now hold the tool in your hand and imagine the helpful faeries. Merge with the faery energy and use your deep breathing and intention to move that image and power into the tool. Your Faery Magick tool is now ready to use.

Faery Magick Spell and Ritual Basics

Of primary importance in Faery Magick is going outdoors and communing with the faeries' home (Nature). You can go to a secluded spot were no one else goes, to the ocean, a mountain, a lake, a nearby park, or you can go out in your backyard.

When you work with the faeries, **never** carry or wear iron or steel. Check your jewelry, shoe and belt buckles, buttons on your clothes, and so forth. Also, make sure you are gracious and completely honest with the faeries, or they won't help you or grant you favors and gifts.

Before making magick, you need to set up your altar with your Faery Magick tools and other focal items, such as candles, incense, and flowers. Also write down the spell that you are doing in your Faery Magick journal (Book of Shadows). Make a note of the date, time, day of the week, and moon phase for future reference. Next create your Faery Ring and magick Circle. Then, call in the faery guardians and invite the helpful Earth, Air, Fire, and Water faeries into your Circle. After you have done these things, it is time for magick-making and spellcasting. After you are done, bid farewell to the helpful faeries (the faery guardians), pull up the Circle and put your tools away.

Always keep in mind that successful Faery Magick stems from your intention, together with your expectation, desire, and how deep you merge with the divine faery beings. In this way, you conceive, create, and experience your magickal goals to the fullest. Make every effort to fully understand your intention, and that you really want what you are seeking to attain. You need to have an especially strong desire to achieve your magickal goal. Most important of all is the depth of your merge with the helpful faery powers. To merge deeply, imagine that you are becoming one with the helpful faeries. Often, merging is accompanied by a feeling of euphoria, deep relaxation, spinning, floating, and flying sensations, heaviness, or light-headedness. When you merge, you bridge the gap between the mortal and faery worlds.

When doing Faery Magick, make sure your magickal goals are clear, concise, and simple. Choosing, creating, and enacting your magickal goals is what magick is all about.

Creating the Faery Ring

After you have set up your altar, you then create the Faery Ring. To do this, tie a loop on each end of your 9-ft. cord. Then slip the point of your athame through the loop, and stick it into the ground where the center of the Circle is to be. Put the index finger of your power hand through the loop on the opposite end of the cord and gently stretch it out. Holding the cord, now walk clockwise in a circle, dragging your heel to mark the outline of the circle. Then walk clockwise around the circle and lay flowers or herbs on top of the circle outline. You have now created a faery ring.

Creating the Faery Magic Circle

The Faery Magick Circle protects you from harmful energies when doing magick. It acts as a vortex of light, bridging the mortal and faery worlds. Each time you do magick, you create the magick Circle. First, sprinkle water from your cup clockwise all around the inside of the Faery Ring to purify the area. Then hold your athame or wand in your power hand with the point outward, face in the direction North of your Faery Ring, and slowly spin in a clockwise circle. As you do this imagine a blue-white light shooting out of its tip. Trace a clockwise circle of light with your athame over the Faery Ring you have created. You are basically drawing a double circle. Next, face the altar, and say:

> *"I consecrate this Circle of power*
> *To the generous and helpful faeries*
> *Of Earth, Air, Fire, and Water.*
> *May they bless this circle with their presence.*
> *So be it! Blessed be!"*

Calling in the Faery Guardians

Once you have created the Faery Ring and magick Circle, it is time to invoke the faery guardians to protect the Elemental gates of your sacred space. They guard the thresholds of each of the Four Directions and remain there until you release them. From the earth come the gnomes, garden and forest faeries and dryads; from the Air come the winged sylphs; from the Fire come the salamanders; and from the Water come the merrows and the undines.

Face the Northern point of your Circle, ring the bell three times, and merge with the Earth faeries. These are the underground and surface Earth beings, such as the dryads which are tall; green and brown tree spirits; garden and woodland faeries who love the dawning sun and are brown or green, small, and often winged, who love music and dancing; gnomes who are short, squat, with large arms, and live under rocks; leprechauns; and brownies. Earth faeries live in trees, in tall grasses, and at the gnarled base of old trees. As you merge with the Earth faeries, say:

"Helpful faeries of the North march.
Generous faeries of Earth
Come, I pray you.
Protect the gate of the North Ward,
And guard this Circle and all within
Come, I welcome you!"

Face East, ring the bell three times, and merge with the Air faeries. These are the lovely winged sylphs who are often surrounded by a radiant glow, and the weather faeries, such as wind faeries, which influence storms whose, wings are usually larger than their bodies. As you merge with the Air faeries, say:

"Helpful faeries of the East march.
Generous faeries of Air,
Come, I pray you.
Protect the gate of the East Ward,
And guard this Circle and all within.
Come, I welcome you!"

Face South, ring the bell three times, and merge with the Fire faeries. These are the Fire spirits and salamanders who represent the destructive and creative power of fire. Every time a fire is lit, a Fire faery is present. As you merge with the Fire faeries, say:

> *"Helpful Faeries of the South march.*
> *Generous faeries of Fire,*
> *Come, I pray you.*
> *Protect the gate of the South Ward,*
> *And guard this Circle and all within.*
> *Come, I welcome you!"*

Face West, ring the bell three times, and merge with the Water faeries. They are the salt Water faeries, such as the merrows; and sprites who are playful and active, and often look very human-like with webbed feet and hands. Fresh water faeries, such as the undines, are dreamlike and beautiful, with enchanting voices. They live in ponds, rivers, and lakes. As you merge with the Water faeries, say:

> *"Helpful Faeries of the West march.*
> *Generous faeries of Water,*
> *Come, I pray you.*
> *Protect the gate of West Ward,*
> *And guard this Circle and all within.*
> *Come, I welcome you!"*

Now stand in the center of your magick Circle, ring the bell three times, and say:

> *"Helpful faeries of Earth, Air, Fire, Water, and Spirit*
> *Come. I pray you.*
> *Grant me your divine power and protection tonight!*
> *So be it! Blessed be!"*

The faery guardians are now in place.

Cutting the Energy Door

After you set the faery guardians in place, cut an energetic doorway from which you can enter and exit the

Circle without disrupting its magickal energy. Traditionally this is done just below the Eastern most point of your Circle, but for practical purposes you can also cut the doorway at the actual doorway in the room. Use your athame to cut the doorway by tracing a doorway with it. Each time you exit and re-enter your Circle, open and close the doorway with a sweeping motion of your athame.

Bidding Farewell to the Faery Guardians

Once you are done with your Faery Magick spells and other works, bid farewell to the faery guardians. Face the Northern most point of the Circle, ring the bell once, and say:

> *"Generous faeries of Earth, I bid you farewell.*
> *Depart in peace and love.*
> *Many thanks for your presence."*

Face East, ring the bell, and say:

> *"Generous faeries of Air, I bid you farewell.*
> *Depart in peace and love.*
> *Many thanks for your presence."*

Face South, ring the bell once, and say:

> *"Generous faeries of Fire, I bid you farewell.*
> *Depart in peace and love.*
> *Many thanks for your presence."*

Face West, ring the bell once, and say:

> *"Generous faeries of Water, I bid you farewell.*
> *Depart in peace and love.*
> *Many thanks for your presence."*

Stand at the center of the Circle and ring the bell once, and say:

"So be it! Blessed be!"

Pulling Up the Faery Magick Circle and Ring

Once you have bidden farewell to the faery guardians, it is time to pull up the magick Circle and Faery Ring. Do so by holding your athame or wand in your power hand, face North, and slowly turn in a counterclockwise circle. As you do this, imagine the blue-white light of the Circle being drawn back up into your athame or wand. Then scatter the flowers in the ring to and fro, and erase the mark of the ring with your shoe, foot, or besom. Do this in a counterclockwise motion. Lastly, ring the bell once, and say:

"The Circle is open, but ever unbroken.
May peace and love fill our hearts.
Merry meet, merry part, and merry meet again!
Blessed be!"

Now clap your hands three times. It is done.

Romance and Love

Once upon a time, a widow with a farm at Blaensawde, near Mydffai, Wales, sent her only son a few miles up the valley to graze their cattle on the shores of a beautiful lake called Llyn y Van Ffach. One sunny day, after kissing his widowed mother goodbye, her son began the two-mile trek up through the valley to a lake, where the cattle could graze all day long on the fertile grass that grew at the edge of the water.

While eating his lunch, the young man saw a dazzling faery lake maiden. He watched as she combed her long blond curls, using the glass-like surface of the lake as her mirror. Instantly, he fell in love with her, and in doing so he held out his arms to her, beseeching her to come ashore. Still in his hands was the bread that he had been eating. Staring at him, she said, "Your bread is too hard." She then swam back into the depths of the lake, leaving the herds-man mystified.

Returning to his mother, he told her the story of the faery maiden. In response, his sympathizing mother gave him a loaf of bread that had not been baked at all, and the next day he went back to the lake.

The faery maiden reappeared from the lake, and this time she said, "Your bread is baked too soft."

He returned to his mother, and she responded by baking him a loaf that was neither too hard nor too soft. The next day, he again returned to the side of the lake. The faery responded by telling him, "Your bread is baked just right." He then had passed the first part of the mythical test given to mortals who fall in love with faeries.

Next, a noble elderly man rose from the depths of lake with an identical twin at his left side and at his right side, both looking like the faery maiden of the herdsman's dreams. The older man told him that he had to choose the correct maiden. He looked at both with confused wonder, each looking like the other. He was just about to give up and guess when one of the faery maidens moved her foot slightly. When she did so, he saw the bindings on her sandals matched his memories of his true love.

He chose the correctc maiden, resulting in a very large dowry of land, a house, the many fine heirlooms passed down from generation to generation, and as many cattle as the faery maiden could count in one breath—and she counted extremely fast. The only catch was that he must never give the faery maiden three causeless blows, otherwise he would lose her and the dowry. The couple lived happily ever after, producing three bountiful boys.

This story is called "Undine's Kymric Sisters" presented in John Rhy's Celtic Folklore, and is one of the best-known and *earliest Welsh folk faery tales. Indeed, the faery tales of the Lake Maidens, who are neither sirens nor nixies who married mortals, are among the most well known. This particular story is considered to be based in fact and happened in the 12th century at a small lake near the Black Mountains.*

This Welsh faery tale is one of the many in which faeries take mortal lovers. Oftentimes there is an attraction, a divine union, that energetically moves beyond the continuum of what is "now." In modern New Age terminology, the union in love of two beings—mortal and faery—likely represents key components in both the mortal's and faery's spiritual evolution.

As are humans, the faeries are preoccupied with love. Love and romance is to life what spices are to cooking. You can live without spice, but when you do, life is bland and flat. With love and romance in your life, it becomes a feast that has depth and can be savored with each new day (and night). In this way, love and romance are elements that help make life an adventure rather than an arduous and painstaking journey. Love and romance give a child-like excitement to life much like the faeries themselves. This is why the two go together so well.

The Faery Magick spells and journeys in this chapter focus on using Faery Magick in love and romance. The items you will need are listed first and then each step of the procedure is explained. Whenever possible, do Faery Magick in Nature. When you are done, make certain that you pull up the Faery Magick Ring and Circle. Also make every effort to keep sacred spaces outdoors as Natural and beautiful as possible. This will help attract the faeries to your sacred space again and again.

Before starting, you need to attract helpful faeries into your Faery Magick Ring and Circle. The best way to do this is through your intention, expectation, desire, merging with the faery energies, and a little ingenuity.

To get to know the faery folk, frequent the places in Nature where they dwell. Look in oak groves and in old oak and alder trees. Look in caves or holes in the ground, in fountains, by rivers, creeks, and streams, or by lakes and ponds. Look within Natural rings of mushrooms, grasses, or flowers just before the sun goes down, in the full moon light, or at dawn.

Gain faery favors and gifts by making heartfelt offerings to the faeries. For example, put crystals and stones in places where you look for faeries in Nature as a gift for the faeries. Traditionally, stones such as moonstone, clear and milky quartz crystal, rose quartz, amethyst, aquamarine, emerald, and staurolite, are preferred by the helpful and generous faeries.

Another way of attracting helpful faery beings are by planting flowers, trees, and vegetables in your garden. They love roses, lavender, hollyhocks, petunias, and many others (refer to Chapter 4 for a list of faery flowers). Also, keep living flowers and plants inside your home to encourage faery energies. Use scented oils, such as rose or potpourri. Place a tabletop fountain in your sacred space, or build a small waterfall and pool in your backyard. Create a faery habitat with flowers that attract butterflies and dragonflies, ladybugs, and honey bees. And remember to put treats, such as milk, honey, bread, and cakes, out at night as offerings to the faeries (they enjoy the essence of the offering, without actually eating it).

Faery Tree Spell

All trees have a spirit or dryad within them. You can commune with the dryads of trees, and ask them for faery gifts and favors. Never carve runes into living trees as it often harms them and angers the dryad within. Instead, trace initials, runes, and other magickal symbols on trees and other living things with scented oils. Use consecrated oils associated with the faeries such as amber, rose, and lavender, when doing Faery Magick. The Elemental energies of the consecrated oils combine with the faery energies to create powerful magick. Do this spell in early Spring, on a sunny day during a waxing moon when the fruit trees are blossoming. You can do this spell by yourself, or you can do it with your beloved.

✳ A blossoming fruit tree
   (apple, cherry, apricot, plum, nectarine, peach, or pear).

✳ Amber-scented oil.

1.   Find a blossoming fruit tree, and walk around it clockwise three times. As you do, softly chant:

"Spirit of the tree, blessed be!"

2.   Use the scented oil to anoint yourself (and your beloved), and then trace your initials and your beloved's initials on the tree trunk. Trace over them three times with the oil. Draw a heart around your initials, and then trace six five-pointed stars around the heart.

3.   Put both your hands on the tree, and say:

"Beautiful blossoming fruit tree
Bless us with your love so sweet
Young and old, strong and free,
By the Divine Spirit of this tree,
So be it! Blessed be!"

4.   Now walk around the tree clockwise six more times, all the while chanting:

"Spirit of the tree, blessed be!"

Faery Feather Charm

The birds are often said to be the faeries in disguise. Most likely, when you have been out in Nature, you have

happened upon a bird feather on the ground, a bush, or tree. These feathers are little faery gifts that can lead you to higher and more fulfilling love. The magickal meanings of these feathers is determined by their colors as follows: **(Note: Bird feathers may carry disease, so be careful to clean your feathers and your hands when handling them.)**

White: Birth, initiation, love, joy, purity.

Blue: A gift, love, happiness.

Green: Magick, adventure, dreams, prosperity, new ventures.

Rose: Romance, love, spiritual union.

Red: Magick, good luck, love, passion, fortune.

Yellow: Friendship, fellowship, companionship.

Orange: Happiness to come in the future.

Brown: Good health, happy home, good fortune.

Gray: Peace of mind, tranquility, harmony, wisdom.

Blue and White: A new love, a love affair.

Brown and White: Good health and much happiness.

Gray and White: A new and happy event or situation.

Make this Faery Feather Charm on or just before a full moon to help your love life soar to new heights.

* White or blue fresh flowers.
* A white or blue feather.
* Jasmine-scented oil.
* A photo of yourself.
* A photo of the one you love.
* A rose-colored pouch.

1. After the moon rises, take everything you need for the charm and go outdoors. You can also do this work near a picture window where you can see the moon.

2. Draw a Faery Magick Ring, and scatter the fresh flowers clockwise around the Ring. Then, draw a Magick Circle, and call in the faery guardians.

3. Anoint yourself with the scented oil, and then anoint the feather with the oil. Put the feather in the pouch, and then add the photos, so that they face each other, with the feather positioned between them.

4. Close the pouch, anoint it with the scented oil. Empower it by holding it in your hands, and saying three times:

> *"Winged faeries, blessed be*
> *May my love fly to me.*
> *By North, East, South, and West,*
> *May our love be divinely blessed."*

5. When you are done, thank the winged faeries, bid farewell to the faery guardians, and pull up the Circle.

6. Put the charm under your mattress or bed to bring more joy and love into your life. Recharge it once a month by anointing it with the jasmine oil, holding it in your hands, and repeating:

> *"Winged faeries, blessed be*
> *May my love fly to me.*
> *By North, East, South, and West,*
> *May our love be divinely blessed."*

Puff-Ball Faery Wish

Children and adults alike enjoy making wishes by blowing on puff-balls. Use this fun and easy faery wish to make your most cherished love wish come true:

+ Fresh flowers.
+ A love wish.
+ A dandelion that has seeded into a puff-ball.

1. Pick the puff-ball on the night of a full moon in the spring or summer.

2. Set up your Faery Magick Ring, and scatter the fresh flowers around it clockwise. Then draw your Faery Magick Circle, and call in the faery guardians.

3. Focus on the various aspects of your wish–the touch, the smell, the color, the size, and so forth. The more definitive you are in what you want, the more chance you have of getting it.

4. Now go to each of the Four Directions, beginning with the North point. Holding the puff ball in your right hand say:

> *"Oh great and shining powers of the faery,*
> *Let your loving energies fill this seed*
> *In the name of the generous faeries, blessed be!"*

5. Upon returning again to the North point, use your breath to blow the spores from the stem, and as you do so, imagine your wish becoming part of the wind and the over-all Elements. Feel the power of the faery coming into the Circle, helping your wish to come true.

6. When you are done, thank the faeries, bid farewell to the faery guardians, and pull up the circle.

Faery May Day Journey

There are differnt ways to do the journeys in this book They are as follows:

✴ Read the journeys to yourself. Close your eyes, and imagine what you have read. Make sure you go over each sentence in your mind's eye before moving to the next one.

✴ Tape-record the journeys in your own voice, and then listen to them when you like. (Do not read the numbers when you tape record the journey). This is probably the most effective way to do the journeys as you can play the tape again and again, yet surprisingly each time the journey is fresh and new.

✳ Have your beloved read the journeys to you, taking plenty of time for each sentence. This will give *you* ample time to imagine the steps of the journey. (Note: Do not drive, ride a bike, jog, operate or machinery (including our computer), do other activities when you are doing the journeys. Your attention needs to be focused on the task at hand.)

✳ A piece of tumbled clear quartz.

✳ A place in Nature.

1. Go outdoors at noon on May Day. Pick a spot where you won't be interrupted or distracted. If you decide to do the journey indoors, turn on some soft faery-like music to accompany the journey. This will help you enter a more relaxed state of mind, which is especially conducive to visualization.

2. Get as comfortable as you can. Close your eyes, and inhale deeply, and then exhale completely. Now, imagine breathing in green light, and breathing out any stress or worries you may have. Next, take a deep breath, tighten the muscles in your body, and then exhale and let your body go limp. Do this three times. Continue to breathe deeply and completely, allowing yourself to become more relaxed. Think about how your body is naturally and rhythmically breathing by itself. You feel serene and calm, yet peacefully aware.

3. Shift your body slightly to get even more comfortable. Then with your eyes still closed, imagine a single point of green light, backed in black. The single point of light becomes brighter and larger. Imagine moving your awareness toward the light. The emerald green radiance is warm and inviting as you move closer and closer. As you reach the emerald green light, you feel as though you become one

with it, merging completely. You are the light; the light is you. You are one.

4. Consciously stepping into the light, you are transported to a magickal wooded place in Nature. Next to you is your lover (or your future lover). Directly in front of the two of you is a Natural stairway made of Earth and lined with flowers of every color. The stairway leads to a clearing in the woods. Taking your beloved's hand, you move together down the nine earthen steps, one at a time. The flower fragrances strong, you notice the flowers seem to move and shift like tiny dancing faeries as you walk down the steps. You both pause to watch them in wonder for a few minutes, and then continue on.

The sun smiles upon you; its rays caress your skin like warm, golden fingers. Your lover's fingers slip through yours as you walk along. Everything glimmers, basking in the bright sunlight, and the colors of the woods seem more vibrant, just like they do right after a rainstorm. In the tree canopy above, the birds sing. You walk through a patch of golden marigolds, and you suddenly understand the language of the birds as they frolic and sing.

Now, imagining a loving and enchanting embrace with your beloved, resume your adventures through the magickal woods. You come to a small meadow covered with a blanket of green grass. A gentle breeze ripples through the grass. Tiny dots of white daisies bloom from out of the fertile earth. You watch as the flowers move on their own accord in the breeze. They dance a slow and graceful circle dance around the meadow, around you and your beloved. You can hear a tune in the gentle breeze, but you can't quite make out the melody. You both watch a magnificent white stag dance and prance across the meadow, in synch with the dancing flowers. He meets a young doe at its edge, and the deer dance together into the depths of the woods. You can hear the crackling and crunching as they move through the forest.

You and your beloved sit down in the grassy meadow. You notice a wild strawberry patch next to you. Your love sees the fruit at the same time, reaches over and picks a berry, and feeds it to you, slowly and sensuously. Your teeth sink down into the succulent fruit and it fills your senses as you close your eyes and enjoy the berry. Opening your eyes, you pick a berry and feed it to your beloved. You both stretch out and watch a giant swallowtail butterfly float above you. In a flash, the butterfly transforms into a beautiful winged faery, who hovers over you and waves what looks like a magick wand. You see a bright wave of golden stars come from the tip of the wand and drift down upon your and your beloved. You feel as though you have been filled with pure love and bliss.

The faery beckons you both to follow, and you come to a place where a narrow stream diverges into two, and then back into one. The two streams surround a small island. The butterfly faery flits over to a large gnarled oak that grows from the center of the island. You both hop over the narrow stream, and go over to the oak. As you do, the dryad of the oak greets you. She flows out of the trunk of the tree, standing more than 9 feet tall and growing all the time. Her hair is greenish-brown, and flows all around the tree. She smiles at you, and as you look into her eyes, you are filled with a warm emerald green light. Your beloved embraces you once again, lovingly and sensuously, and instantly you find yourself once again at the bottom of the nine Earthen steps lined with flowers of every color.

5. Take your lover's hand, and move up the steps. With each step you take, you feel more refreshed and energized, remembering everything that is important from your journey. As you reach the top of the steps, imagine stepping back through the emerald light, into the present time and place.

6. Slowly open your eyes, and move your fingers and toes. Stretch your body like a cat, and then clap your hands together

three times. You can repeat this journey as many times as you like. Each time, it will be an original magickal adventure.

Rose Faery Love Blessing

The faeries, flowers, and magick are interwoven in a rich and ancient tapestry. As the queen of faery flowers, the rose is the universal symbol of love. The ultimate flowering of the spirit, the rose symbolizes matter made divine. In Roman mythology, Flora, the flower goddess, pleaded with the other gods and goddesses to turn her immortal essence into the mortal rose after the death of her favorite nymph.

This Rose Faery Love Blessing uses the divine essence of the rose to protect and bless those you love. You can do the blessing alone or in the presence of a loved one, any evening you like. For the strongest power, say this blessing on Midsummer's Eve. For the best results, use a fresh rose from your garden, a neighbor's garden (with permission), or a wild rose from Nature.

+ A small piece of rose quartz.
+ One rose (pink, peach, or red).
+ A clean sheet of white paper.
+ A 9-in. length of pink ribbon.
+ Rose-scented oil.

1. Just before dusk when the crickets are silent, walk backwards very slowly and quietly toward a specific rosebush. Spin clockwise three times, and then face the bush. Spend a few minutes just tuning into the beauty of the roses, smelling their fragrant and heady scent. Feel the soft, velvety petals of the roses.

2. Snip off one rose from the bush. Thank the rose faeries, and then take the rose inside and place it on your altar.

3. Draw your Faery Magick Ring and Circle and call in the faery guardians. If you are doing this faery blessing with your lover, then invite him or her into your Circle now.

4. Place the rose and the piece of rose quartz on the sheet of paper. Roll them loosely up in the paper. Then secure the paper with the pink ribbon, knotting the ribbon three times.

5. Put a drop of rose essential oil on each of the three knots in the ribbon. Hold the paper with the rose in your power hand, and have your loved one place his or her hand on top of yours. If you are doing this blessing in the absence of your loved one, then visualize your beloved for a few minutes while holding the paper with the rose and stone. Say this blessing aloud to your loved one,:

"Each dawn, morning, day, and eve,
Every night and midnight of your life,
May the love and affection of the Earth faeries be with you,
May the love and affection of the winged faeries be with you,
May the love and affection of the light faeries be with you,
May the love and affection of the Water faeries be with you,
May the love and affection of the helpful fairies be with you.
May they lead you into romance, love, and sweet passion,
And bless and guide you into the Divine loving light.
By the power of the loving Sidhe, Blessed be!"

6. Thank the rose faeries for their love and blessings, and then pull up the Circle and release the guardians. Put the paper with the rose and stone in a safe place until Yule (Winter Solstice).

7. During Yule, take the rose out carefully and place it over your heart. Visualize your loved one, silently telling them that you love him or her. Say the blessing again to your beloved.

8. When you are finished, place the rose under the bush you took it from, and bury the piece of rose quartz at its base as an offering to the fae. Thank the rose faeries for their love, blessings, and affection.

Blessed Fae Picnic

There is nothing quite so romantic as a picnic out in a secluded spot in Nature with your lover. Spending time together, just the two of you in a Natural setting, inspires romantic interludes and sweet, loving memories. Sitting back under the blue sky on a sunny day with the one you love can be pure bliss, far away from daily hassles and stress. In Nature, love and romance are always more exciting and enchanting, and food always seems to taste better. Have this Faery Love picnic on a Friday with your lover to share a few romantic hours together, and to bless and sweeten your love life with a little Faery Magick.

+ Fresh flowers.

+ Honeysuckle oil.

+ A picnic lunch.

+ A blanket.

1. On a sunny afternoon, gather together your picnic lunch (include plenty of love foods, such as strawberries, apples, pears, oranges, peaches, and grapes), a couple of bottles of water, a bottle of chilled sparkling cider or champagne, a blanket, and your beloved, and head out into Nature for a picnic. Find a nice, secluded spot.

2. Before you spread out your blanket and begin eating, draw a Faery Ring, and scatter the fresh flowers, clockwise, around it. Then spread out your blanket inside the faery ring. Anoint each other with the honeysuckle oil on the Third Eye to promote spiritual love. As you do so, say:

"Starspun fae of the North, East, South, and West
May our love be divinely blessed. So be it!"

3. Now, unpack your picnic, and eat it, savoring each bite and each sip. Toast to one another, to the love you share, to a loving today and tomorrow together.

4. Stay until the sunset, talking with each other, embracing, kissing, and holding each other. Use your imagination. Share as much as you can, building a magickal bond that unites your bodies, minds, and souls.

5. Before you leave your picnic spot, drip six drops of the honeysuckle oil inside the Faery Ring as an offering to the Nature faeries, and say:

"Starspun fae of the North, Eeast, South, and West
Thank you for your blessings. Blessed be!"

6. Then pick up the flowers from your Faery Ring and toss them here and there. Pick up all of your trash and leave the picnic spot as undisturbed and Natural as possible.

Pansy Honey Magick

The root of word "pansy" stems from the French "pensee," meaning "thought," because it was believed that pansies could be used to make your beloved think of you, and visa versa. You can use the love power of pansies in this pansy honey to encourage thoughts of love and desires. The flowers are edible and high in vitamins C and A. Make the honey on a Friday, on, or close to, a new moon. Be sure to use the honey up within 30 days for the best results.

* 1/2 cup of fresh, finely chopped pansy petals.
* A bowl.
* A jar of honey.
* A pot of warm water.

1. First, warm the jar of honey by putting it in a pot of warm water for a few minutes.

2. Put the petals in the bowl, and use your fingers to mix them for a few minutes. As you do this, empower the petals by chanting:

"I empower these petals with thoughts of
loving harmony."

3. Add the empowered petals to the jar of honey. Hold the jar of honey between your hands, and say:

"I empower this honey with thoughts of
loving harmony."

4. Put the jar in a pot of warm water and slowly simmer for about 30 minutes, and then allow the honey to cool. Store the pansy honey for about two weeks to strengthen its flavor and magickal power.

5. Make a cup of tea, and add three teaspoons of the pansy honey. As you stir the honey into the tea, say:

"I call upon the flower faeries
Bring thoughts of loving harmony.
Sweet fae honey of romance and beauty
Bring sweet love with each new day."

6. Then go outside, and make an offering of the pansy honey to the flower faeries. Drip nine drops of honey on the ground outside near the entrance of your home, and say:

"I thank the helpful flower faeries
For their thoughts of loving harmony.
Sweet fae honey of romance and beauty,
Bring sweet love with each new day."

Strawberry Love Offering

The strawberry represents passion, rewards, special gifts, and temptation. It is used to invoke love or as an ingredient in love potions. It is good in spells of enticement, and the strawberry is a good gift to the faeries. Make this offering on a Friday:

+ 9 fresh strawberries.

+ Strawberry-scented votive candle.

1. Take the strawberries outdoors with you. Draw a Faery Ring and Circle, and call in the faery guardians.

2. Cup the strawberries in your hands, and empower them by saying three times:

> *"May these berries be divinely blessed*
> *With the loving gifts of the faeries*
> *From North, East, South, and West."*

3. Now eat four of the strawberries, one at the North point of your Faery Circle, one at the East point, one at the South point, and one at the West point.

4. Place the other five berries on the ground around your Circle; at the North, East, South, West, and center points as an offering to the faeries. Stand at the center of the Circle, and say:

> *"I offer these sweet berries*
> *To the helpful and generous faeries*
> *From North, East, South, and West.*
> *In the name of the shining fae,*
> *May my love be divinely blessed."*

5. Bid farewell to the faery guardians, and pull up your Circle. Leave the strawberries where the are.

6. Go back indoors, and light the candle. Dedicate it to the helpful faeries. As you gaze into the candlelight, imagine the helpful faeries bringing you more sweet and shining love every day and night. Allow the candle to burn safely down.

Faery Lavender Love Gift

The helpful flower faeries can add fragrance and beauty to your love life. Flower faeries are probably the easiest to commune with as you just need some living flowers. Lavender is a faery favorite of the winged and garden faeries. It is well-known for its magickal properties of love, devotion, peaceful dreams, harmony, and protection from negativity. Make this love gift on a Friday, on (or just before) a full moon:

* A pot lavender or a lavender bush.
* 1/2 cup dried lavender.
* Lavender essential oil.
* A white pouch.
* Two 12-inch pieces of lavender ribbon.
* A book of love poems.
* A bottle of champagne or sparkling cider.

1. Draw your Faery Ring around a living lavender bush outside, or a pot of lavender. Then draw a Faery Circle, and call in the faery guardians.

2. Ask the lavender plant for six sprigs, and then snip them off. Thank the plant, and set the sprigs aside.

3. Put the dried lavender in the pouch, and add 6 drops of lavender oil to the pouch.

4. Close the pouch, and tie it with one of the pieces of lavender ribbon. Knot the ends three times. With each knot you tie, say:

> "I empower these flowers
> With love, devotion, and harmony
> By the flower faeries, blessed be!"

5. Now tie the other piece of ribbon around the sprigs of fresh lavender. Hold the tied lavender in your power hand, and repeat:

> *"I empower these flowers*
> *With love, devotion, and harmony*
> *By the flower faeries, blessed be!"*

6. Put the tied lavender into the book of love poems. Use the lavender bouquet to mark a favorite poem, one that you want your beloved to read first.

7. When you are done, thank the flower faeries, bid farewell to the faery guardians, and close the Circle.

8. That night, give your lover the book of poems with the lavender sprigs tucked inside, plus the bottle of bubbly (to be shared with your beloved) as a love gift.

9. Put the pouch under your bed, or tuck it into your pillowcase. Also anoint yourself with the lavender oil, and rub your wood furniture with a few drops, especially your bed, bedside table, and bedroom dresser, to promote loving dreams and blissfully romantic nights.

Home and Hearth

Once upon a time, long, long, before you were born, behind the Ochil hills in a lonely and remote spot lived an old woman named Bessie and her little grandchild named Nelly. The old woman kept a cow and some chickens, so that she and Nelly had plenty of milk, butter, and eggs.

Bessie homeschooled little Nelly, teaching her the letters of the alphabet and how to sew a sampler, a piece of canvas stretched over a wooden frame on which is sewn the letters of the alphabet, the numbers 1, 2, 3, 4, 5, 6, 7, 8, 9, and 0, and the person's name (which in this case was Nelly Henderson).

On the long winter nights, Bessie would tell little Nelly wonderful stories about the faeries and brownies, who dwelled in the large earth mound, called The Fairy Knowe, which was near Pendreich, overlooking the beautiful vale of Menteith, and the western group of the Grampian mountains. There they held high revels, dancing in the silver moonbeams, and playing leapfrog and other funny games, which kept them amused until the dawn drove them into hiding.

Little Nelly loved to hear the tales of the faeries, or grey people, as they were also called. She especially loved the story about the tiny elf named Tod Lowrie, or Red Bonnett, *a brownie who wore a red cap. The good-natured and kindly Tod Lowrie was a favorite of the Ochil's shepherd who never spoke an evil word about this "good faery," as he always helped them, though he was never seen by any of them.*

As time went on and Nelly grew older, she wished more than anything else to see her favorite faery, Tod Lowrie, but she never managed to catch even a glimpse of his red cap. Nelly knew that when all the folks in a house were sound asleep, then it was that Tod Lowrie would step inside, and take up the broom and sweep the floors and lay the fire, and leave everything tidy and neat.

One night, Nelly sat by the fire watching the glowing peats, and she prayed to see the brownie Tod Lowrie. Bessie hadn't been feeling very well that day, and Nelly had tried her best to do the work of the house, but she couldn't finish it all. Tired, she slipped into bed with her grandmother, and immediately fell asleep. It was the month of January, and the winter temperature was severe, and the ground was covered with snow.

A snowstorm began to blow across the moor just as the evening shadows began to fall. Soon after Nelly feel asleep, the door gently opened, and a strange, quaint little figure stole into the room. It was a wee man with a red cap upon his head, green shoes upon his feet, and a tight little jacket of greenish leather closely buttoned round his body. He glanced around the room; the only light to be seen was from the flickering embers of the peat fire. Having satisfied himself that the household was asleep, he picked up a broom and set to work to sweep the hearth and the floor, and put the dishes on the shelves of the cupboard. Then, Tod Lowrie, went outside to an outhouse and brought in two wooden pitchers full of water, and set them carefully in a corner. Going out again, he brought in some peats, which he placed upon the fire, and bending down upon his knees, he blew the embers until the fire blazed quite cheerily. Taking a hurried glance around again, he was satisfied that all was well. He went in the scullery, and carried a pot into the room, and, having put some water into it, he hung it upon the hook above the fire. The Brownie then took a bowl full of meal, and with a wooden stick called a "spurtle" in his hand, he let the oatmeal trickle through his fingers into the pot, stirring the contents until it boiled. Adding a pinch of salt, he let the pot boil for some time. Then taking out the wooden spurtle, he scraped it upon the side of the pot and laid it carefully aside. He then fetched two wooden bowls from a press, one large and one small.

Turning to the fire, he unhooked the pot, carried it carefully to the table, and poured out the porridge into the two empty bowls. When this was done, Tod Lowrie took the pot into the scullery and washed it clean, using a bunch of heather stalks tied firmly together, called a "range." He went into the scullery again, and returned with two small bowls of fresh milk, which he placed beside the bowls of steaming porridge.

Looking at his handiwork, the brownie smiled to himself and rubbed his hands together in glee. "This will surprise my little Nell," he said to himself. Wheeling around, he said, "Now it's time I was off, before the morning light awakens up my little friend." Tod Lowrie went to the door, but to his great surprise, during the night, the snow had been falling and the wind had been causing it to drift. The snow cover was so thick that the cottage was completely surrounded by a bank of snow, heaped up to the roof. He tried the window next, but it was blocked too. The wee man could find no exit that way. Standing in the middle of the floor, the brownie considered what he should do. At last he hit upon a plan of escape. He went to the fireplace and prepared to climb up the chimney, but as he stepped upon *the jamb of the fireplace, the smoke from the burning peat tickled his little nose and he gave a huge sneeze and fell with a bang onto the floor. The noise woke Nelly from her sleep, and looking out from her box-bed, she saw the wee Brownie with his red cap and green shoes. Thrilled with delight, she cried to Bessie, "Oh look, Granny, here's Tod Lowrie!" But when Granny opened her eyes and looked out of the bed, the Brownie was gone, having leapt up the chimney and vanished. So, after all, the only person who ever saw Tod Lowrie was little Nelly, whose pure eyes and kind heart enabled her to see the good faery.*

Adapted from *Story of the Brownie* by R. Menzies Fergusson, part of the *Ochil Fairy Tales*, this story has been told in many ways, but its essence remains the same. It demonstrates that those of us with pure eyes and kind hearts are more likely to glimpse the helpful faeries as well as gain their favors. So keep your sight clear and keep a gentle heart to help draw the magickal powers of a brownie to your home with the following Brownie Home Magick spell:

Brownie Home Magick

Brownies are helpful faeries about 3 feet tall, with brown faces and shaggy heads, usually dressed in brown. They often adopt a household and come out at night, when the household is asleep to help with chores of milking, shoe-making, harvesting, threshing corn, sewing, shearing, running errands, and cleaning. Brownies are always gone by the first cock call. A brownie will often become personally attached to one person in the family. Attract a helpful brownie to your home by doing this work after dark on a new moon for best results.

* Your faery broom.
* A bowl of milk.
* A plate of sweet cakes with honey.

1. Sweep your hearth clean using your Faery Broom.

2. Then put the bowl of milk and plate of sweet cakes o n or close to the hearth. Say:

> *"I offer these gifts to the helpful brownies."*

3. Now go to sleep.

4. In the morning, take the milk and cakes outside, and return them to the Earth as an offering to the helpful brownies. As you do this, repeat,

> *"I offer these gifts to the helpful brownies."*

5. Repeat this spell once a month to bring the helpful, protective powers of the brownies into your home.

Faery Broom Magick

Use your faery broom to sweep your hearth clean of both debris and unwanted energies. To encourage faery visits and their protection, you must leave your hearth well swept. This ties into the idea that some of the helpful faeries are ancestral spirits who are buried under the hearth, according to ancient custom. Do this spell during a waning moon. Then use your faery broom whenever you want to sweep negativity out and positivity into your home.

* A broom made of wood and broomstraw.
* 12-inch lengths of white, red, and black ribbon.
* 3 rosemary stalks (6 inches long).
* 3 lavender stalks (6 inches long).
* 3 sage stalks (6 inches long).
* Cedar-scented oil.

1. Gather together the items you will need. Then draw a Faery Ring around your hearth, draw a Magick Circle, and call in the faery guardians. (Note: If you don't have a hearth, use your altar area).

2. Braid the three ribbons together, and then knot them on each end. As you do this, chant:

"One, two, three, bring helpful fae energy to me."

3. Use the braided ribbon to tie the lengths of rosemary, lavender, and sage around the broom at the top of the broomstraws. As you do this, call the fae who work with rosemary, lavender, and sage to lend their spiritual energy toward protecting your home from harm and unwanted energies. Say:

"Fae of rosemary, I ask for your protection and blessings.
Fae of lavender, I ask for your protection and blessings.
Fae of sage, I ask for your protection and blessings."

4. Now, think of a name for your Faery Broom. This gives it more power. Use cedar oil to trace the broom's name on its handle with letters, runes, or other magickal symbols. Do this three times. Each time you trace the name, say:

"I consecrate this broom (say the broom's name)
To the helpful and protective faeries.
So be it! Blessed be!"

5. Next, stand in the center of your hearth (or in the center of your Faery Magick Circle if you don't have a hearth). Move clockwise (sunwise), us ing your faery broom to sweep from the center outward. This means you will be sweeping in a complete circle, from the center outward. With each sweeping motion, imagine the area being cleansed of all unwanted energies. Say:

"Blessed and divine Faery Broom,
Sweep out harm, sweep out doom,
Sweep away evil from this hearth and room."

6. Now, stand in the middle of your hearth area, and begin sweeping in positive protective, energy. As you do, say:

"Blessed and divine Faery broom,
Sweep in love, sweep in boons,
Sweep joy into this hearth and room."

Rest your faery broom on the left (Goddess) side of your hearth or altar when you aren't using it. Stand the broom on its handle with the broomstraws up to invite the helpful faeries into your hearth and home.

Musical Faery Wand

At night, the faery hills are ablaze with merrymaking, dancing, and music. Faery music is the finest and the grandest ever heard. Beautiful and sweet, you can hear it on moonlit nights in the hills, canyons, and hollows, or blown in over the water or waves. Great musicians, especially pipers, fiddlers, and harpists, have been inspired by the enchanting music of the faeries.

The sweet-sounding bells on this musical faery wand will attract the creative powers of the helpful faeries. Faery wands are probably the most powerful tools in Faery Magick. Many faery tales include the "waving of the magick wand" scene, where people, animals, and things are magickally transformed.

The musical wand and silver branch are faery favorites. This musical faery wand integrates the two into one powerful Faery Magick tool. It can be used for making magick, shapeshifting, and meditation. The best time to make your wand is at dusk on the eve of one of the eight Sabbats. I suggest that parents and children, and groups of friends make their wands together as part of their Sabbat celebration. It's empowering and fun for everyone!

* A white candle.
* A branch (measuring 13 to 19 inches).
* 9 small golden bells.

* Non-toxic silver paint.
* Paint brush.
* 3 pieces of 18-inch ribbon (red, black, and white).
* Sandalwood incense.
* 3 pinches of rosemary in 1/2 cup of hot water.
* A soft cloth.

1. During the daylight hours, go outdoors and find a tree branch the proper size. Traditionally, branches from hazel trees were used for faery wands, but I have found that oak, apple, mountain ash, birch, madrone, and driftwood also work well. Ideally, the branch should be a dead branch that is lying on the ground, because when something dies in the Earthly realm, it is reborn in the faery realm.

2. At dusk, gather together the items you need to make your wand. Then draw a Faery Magick Circle and call in the faery guardians. Light the candle and incense, dedicating them both to the helpful faeries. Sit or stand comfortably in front of your altar, while gazing at the candlelight. Quietly contemplate the energies you want your musical faery wand to embody. After a few minutes, hold the branch in both hands, and say three times:

"Tree spirit please empower me
In the name of the fae, blessed be!"

3. Next, pass the branch through the incense smoke three times. Apply a little bit of the rosemary water to the cloth, and wipe the branch with it nine times, dipping the cloth into the rosemary water each time. Wipe the branch with the cloth from the base upward toward the point. This empowers the branch with rosemary fae protective energy. Once you are done wiping the branch, pass it through the incense smoke again. Set the branch on the altar for a few minutes to dry.

4. Bathe the paint, paintbrush, nine bells, and pieces of ribbon in the smoke to purify them as well. Then paint the branch silver, and let it dry.

5. Once the paint is dry, tie three bells on each ribbon, and tie the ribbons on the wand, spacing them at least an inch apart. The bells should dangle a little from the wand body so that they can ring freely. Each time you wind the ribbon around the wand body and attach three bells, say three times:

> *"Sweetly singing, helpful faery spirits*
> *Please come into this musical wand now.*
> *By the faeries, blessed be!"*

6. After fastening the ribbons and bells to the musical wand, hold it in both hands. Gaze at the candle flame for a few minutes, once again, quietly contemplating the divine powers of your faery wand.

7. Next, face North and take a deep and complete breath, in and out. Hold the wand in your power hand. Sound the wand by shaking it softly above your head three times, merge with the faery energies of Earth, and say:

> *"Faery powers of Earth, I honor you*
> *And invite you into this wand now.*
> *Blessed be the helpful fae!"*

Face East, take a deep and complete breath in and out. Hold the wand above your head, shake it three times to sound it, merge with the faery energies of Air, and say:

> *"Faery powers of Air, I honor you*
> *And invite you into this wand now.*
> *Blessed be the helpful fae!"*

Face South, take a complete breath in and out. Hold the wand upward, and shake it three times above your head to sound it once again. Merge with the Fire faeries, and say:

> *"Faery powers of Fire, I honor you*
> *And invite you into this wand now.*
> *Blessed be the helpful fae!"*

Face West, take a deep and complete breath in and out. Hold the wand above your head and shake it three times to sound it. Merge with the Water faeries, and say:

> *"Faery powers of Water, I honor you*
> *And invite you into this wand now.*
> *Blessed be the helpful fae!"*

8. Next, hold the base of the wand against your navel, and say:

> *"By the Elemental powers of Earth, Air, Fire, and Sea*
> *By the wisdom and power of the eternal sacred tree*
> *Activate, bless, and protect the creative powers of this wand*
> *By the faeries of North, East, South, and West, blessed be!"*

9. When you are done, bid farewell to the faery guardians, and pull up your Faery Magick Circle. Allow the candle to burn safely down on its own. Put your wand on your Faery Magick altar when you are not using it.

Faery Amulet

Eggs are often used as protective home amulets. Make this protective home amulet just before or on a full moon, or on the Spring Equinox, to give it the most faery power. Again, this spell is one you can enjoy with your children and friends.

* An egg.
* A needle.
* Fresh flowers.
* 1 tsp. dried mint.
* 1 tsp. dried cinnamon.

✳ 1 tsp. caraway seeds.

✳ A small funnel.

✳ A large gold or silver star sticker.

1. Gather everything you will need together and go outside. Draw a Faery Ring and Faery Magick Circle. Lay the fresh flowers clockwise around the ring, and then call in the faery guardians.

2. Sit inside the Circle. Use the needle to make a small hole in the egg. Then use the needle to make the hole big enough to put the end of the small funnel into it. Take your time when doing this. It's a little tricky, so you may have to use more than one egg to perfect your technique. Drain the egg into the earth, under a flower bush, tree, or other plant. As you do this, say:

> *"I offer this to the helpful and protective faeries*
> *Of Earth, Air, Fire, and Water. Blessed be!"*

3. Now, put the funnel up to the opening and fill the egg with the dried herbs and seeds. As you do this, chant:

> *"Faeries of mint, cinnamon, and caraway,*
> *Fill this amulet with your divine power today."*

4. Apply the large star sticker to the opening to close it. After you do this, gently hold the egg in your power hand, and say:

> *"May this divine faery amulet*
> *Protect my home from harm.*
> *By the helpful fae, blessed be!"*

5. When you are finished, thank the helpful faeries, bid farewell to the guardians, and pull up the Circle and erase your Ring.

6. Put the faery amulet on your Faery Magick altar. Empower it every full moon by gently holding it in your power hand, and repeating:

"May this divine faery amulet
Protect my home from harm.
By the helpful fae, blessed be!"

Faery Home Basket

The fragrance of lavender balances, soothes, calms, relaxes, and heals. Lavender essential oil contains the scent, taste, and medicinal properties of the plant itself in a concentrated form. This is why anointing yourself with the oil helps you become one with the lavender flower faery energies. Use fresh tree branches, herbs, grasses, and flowers for this basket to invite the powerful energies of the specific fae they embody. Harvest the fresh items in the morning on a dry day. Cut the stalks in 12-inch lengths, and be sure to thank the helpful faeries. If you like, you can make this faery home basket outdoors with your family and friends.

- An undyed basket made of natural materials.
- 6 small pine branches.
- 6 small cedar branches.
- 6 fresh lavender stalks.
- 6 blades of long wild grass.
- 6 wild flowers.
- 6 rosemary sprigs.
- 36 whole cloves.
- Three 12-in. pieces of silver ribbon.
- Three 12-in. pieces of gold ribbon.
- Lavender essential oil.

1. Gather together all the items you will need. Anoint yourself with the lavender oil, and then anoint the outside of the basket with several drops of the oil.

2. Next, line the basket with the pine and cedar branches. Hold the basket in your hands, and say:

"Please, protect my home, family, and pets from harm
Each and every day and each and every night.
By the powers of the pine and cedar faeries,
By the powers of divine and ancient faery light,
So be it! Blessed be! Blessed be! Blessed be!"

3. Add the lavender stalks and rosemary sprigs to the basket. Now hold the basket in your hands, and say:

"Please, protect my home, family, and pets from harm
Each and every day and each and every night.
By the powers of the lavender and rosemary faeries,
By the powers of divine and ancient faery light,
So be it! Blessed be! Blessed be! Blessed be!"

4. Add the wild grasses and wild flowers, hold the basket in your hands, and say:

"Please protect my home, family, and pets from harm
Each and every day and each and every night.
By the powers of the wild grasses and wild flower faeries,
By the powers of divine and ancient faery light,
So be it! Blessed be! Blessed be! Blessed be!"

5. Sprinkle the cloves into the basket, hold the basket in your hands, and say:

"Please protect my home, family, and pets from harm
Each and every day and each and every night.
By the powers of the fragrant clove faeries,
By the powers of divine and ancient faery light,
So be it! Blessed be! Blessed be! Blessed be!"

6. Tie the gold and silver ribbons on the handle of the basket. As you do, say:

"Please protect my home, family, and pets from harm
Each and every day and each and every night
By the powers of the golden sun and silver moon,
By the powers of the ancient faery light,
So be it! Blessed be! Blessed be! Blessed be!"

7. Now, sprinkle several drops of the lavender essential oil over the contents of the basket. Then, put you faery flower home basket in a place of prominence in your home for 28 days. Its enchanting fragrance will continue to attract the protective and helpful powers of the flower and tree faeries to your home. After 28 days, return the contents of the basket to the earth, and thank the faeries for their protection and help.

Home Harmony Offering

The best way to call in the helpful energies of the faeries is by making them offerings. This spell is designed to bring more harmony and happiness into your home by way of the benevolent Earth, Air, Fire, and Water faeries. After all, harmony is a key to a happy home. Do this spell during a waxing moon.

* Your faery broom.
* 6 pinches of dried nettle (tea bags).
* A white stone.
* A feather.
* An acorn.
* A bottle of water.

1. Gather together the items you will need and go outside either in your front or backyard. Rest your faery broom, with its broomstraws down and handle up, against the back door if you are in your front yard, and against your front

door if you are in the backyard. This protects the other entry from unwanted energies while you are working this spell. Draw a Faery Ring, and sprinkle nettle around the outline of the Ring. Nettle warns of danger and is used to help empower the four wards and protective Circles. Now draw your Faery Magick Circle and call in the faery guardians.

2. Hold the stone in your power hand, and face North. Take a deep, complete breath in and out. Hold the stone on your Third Eye, and merge with the Earth faeries. These are the fae present in each stone and tree, the garden and woodland faeries, the gnomes, drawfs, brownies, and leprechauns. Say:

"I offer this gift to the helpful Earth fae
Please bring harmony and happiness to my home."

Now offer the stone to the earth faeries by placing it gently on the ground in front of you in the North quarter of your Circle.

3. Hold the feather in your power hand, and face East. Take a deep and complete breath, and lightly brush the feather across your face three times, and merge with the air faeries. These are the winged sylphs and weather faeries often surrounded by glowing light. Say:

"I offer this gift to the helpful Air fae
Please bring harmony and happiness to my home."

Now, offer the feather to the fae of the Air by gently tossing the feather into the air toward the East quarter of your Circle.

4. Hold the acorn in your power hand, and face South. Take a deep and complete breath, and hold the acorn on your Third Eye. Merge with the Fire fae. These are the salamanders and Fire spirits that are present in each lit flame. They can add great creative power to your magick. Say:

"I offer this to the helpful Fire fae
Please bring harmony and happiness to my home."

Now, place the acorn in the South quarter of your Circle as an offering to the Fire faeries.

5. Hold the bottle of water in your power hand, and face West. Take a drink of the water. Then, take a deep, complete breath in and out, and then merge with the Water faeries. These are the salt water merrows, mermaids, and sprites, as well as the beautiful and enchanting fresh water undines. Say:

"I offer this gift to the helpful Water fae
Please bring harmony and happiness to my home."

Now pour the water onto the earth in the West quarter of your Circle.

6. Now slowly spin clockwise three times. When you are done spinning, say:

"Helpful fae of Earth, Air, Fire, and Water
Please bring harmony and happiness to my home
From North, East, South, and West, blessed be!"

7. Now sit or stand quietly in the middle of your Circle and imagine the helpful powers of the Earth, Air, Fire, and Water faeries bringing more harmony and joyful happiness to your home forever and a day. Do this for at least 15 minutes.

8. When you are done, thank the helpful faeries of Earth, Air, Fire, and Water, bid farewell to the faery guardians, and pull up the Circle. Be sure to leave the area as beautiful and harmonious as you found it.

9. Go inside and take your faery broom down from the doorway, and put it next to your hearth or altar.

Sweet Rose Faery Potion

Rose faeries are some of my favorite flower faeries. They help with love, healing, and bring good luck and protection to my family and home. We have more than 30 rose bushes, of every kind, planted in our garden, so the rose faeries are ever-present around our home. Make this sweet rose faery potion close to, or on a full moon, for best results.

*(Remember to use caution when ingesting roses, as some of them are **poisonous**.)*

* Uplifting music.
* Food processor.
* 3-quart pyrex or similar pan.
* 2 cups rose petals (unsprayed, centers and stems removed).
* 2 cups spring water.
* 3 1/2 cups sugar.
* 2 tsp. lemon juice.
* 3 oz. liquid pectin.
* Wooden spoon or popsicle stick.

1. Turn on some uplifting music. Next, put the water and rose petals in the food processor, and pulse them a few times to coarsely chop the petals. As you do, say:

> *"Sweet rose faeries, empower this potion*
> *With divine love and protection*
> *So be it! Blessed be!"*

2. Put the mixture into the pan. As you stir the potion, repeat:

> *"Sweet rose faeries, empower this potion.*
> *With divine love and protection*
> *So be it! Blessed be!"*

Bring the mixture to a quick boil, and then turn the heat off. Allow the rose petals to steep in the water for about 20 minutes.

3. Strain the petals, and pour the water into a large bowl. Then return the petals to the earth. As you do, say:

"Rose faeries, thank you for your divine power and sweetness."

4. Put 1 3/4 cups of the rose water into the pan, and then add the sugar. As you stir in the sugar, repeat:

*"Sweet rose faeries, empower this potion
With divine love and protection.
So be it! Blessed be!"*

5. Now add the lemon, and bring the mixture to a hard boil, stirring until you completely dissolve the sugar. As you stir the potion, repeat:

*"Sweet rose faeries, empower this potion
With divine love and protection.
So be it! Blessed be!"*

6. Then add the pectin. Return to a hard boil for exactly one minute, and remove the pan from the heat.

7. While the mixture is hot, Can it in hot, sterilized canning jars. Each time you finish filling a jar, hold it in your hands, and repeat:

*"Sweet rose faeries, empower this potion
With divine love and protection
So be it! Blessed be!"*

Check the seals in your jars once the potion has cooled down.

8. Offer the rose faeries a bit of the potion by dropping a small bit from the tip of a wooden spoon or popsicle stick under each rose bush in your garden. As you do this, say:

"Rose faeries, thank you for your divine power and sweetness."

Then spread the sweet potion on biscuits, bagels, cakes, and toast, and share the food with your family and friends. This will help draw the loving and protective energies of the rose faeries to you, your family, and home.

Faery Tree Talisman

There are many ways to protect yourself from harmful energies and malevolent faeries. For example, you can use sacred symbols such as runes, the pentacle, or the cross, ring bells, whistle, clap your hands, giggle, or laugh. Or you can carry a piece of dry bread in your pocket, hang a stone with a natural hole in it by your front door, leap across southwardly running water, turn your clothes inside out, wear a daisy chain, or carry a four-leaf clover. Trees with red berries, particularly rowan, madrone, and mountain ash, are also used for protection. This faery tree talisman uses the Natural power of a tree to bring more love, good health, protection, and abundance to your home and hearth. Make this talisman at dusk during a waxing moon cycle, preferably on one of the eight Sabbats.

* A nearby tree (you can use living tree in a pot).
* A bowl filled with six handfuls of sweet basil.
* Honeysuckle oil.

1. Select a tree right outside your front door. A yew tree works best. (Note: You can also use a living potted tree.) Commune with the tree dryad by placing both your palms on the tree trunk. Ask the tree if it will help you protect your home from malevolent energies. If you sense a positive response, continue. If not, find another tree to work with.

2. Draw a Faery Ring around the tree. Sprinkle the ring with sweet basil. Then draw your Faery Magick Circle and call in the faery guardians.

3. Now anoint yourself with the honeysuckle oil. Trace the Algiz (Υ) rune (pronounced All-geese) on the tree trunk three times with the oil in the form of a bindrune; one upright, one downward, and one upright again. Algiz is the

rune of defense and protection against invaders, a rune of sanctuary, refuge, and divinity. Each time you trace the rune with the scented oil, say:

"Algiz, Algiz, Algiz
Algiz, Algiz, Algiz
Algiz, Algiz, Algiz,
Blessed be!"

4. Now, place both of your hands on the tree, and imagine the protective energies of the Algiz rune entering the tree. Imagine actually planting the protective runic symbol into the tree. Do this by visualizing a laser beam of rune-shaped light moving from your forehead or your hands into the talisman. Direct your awareness into the tree, and imagine your thought-energy and field of magickal intention being absorbed by the atomic structure of the tree itself. Then address the tree, and galdr Algiz to the tree spirit. Sing:

"Algiz, Algiz, Algiz
Z z z z z z z z z
Uz az iz ez oz
Oz ez iz az uz
Z z z z z z z z z
M m m m m m m m m m."

5. Walk around the tree clockwise nine times. As you do, in your mind's eye imagine a rainbow of colored light radiating from the tree and forming a protective field that extends to the front door of your home. When you are done walking around the tree, place your hands on its trunk once again, and say:

"Blessed be this divine tree.
Please protect my home and stand strong,
Please bless my home and stand long,
By the dryad of the tree, blessed be!"

Now the tree talisman can be used to tap into the protective runic stream of Algiz energy infused into it.

6. When you are done, clap your hands together three times. Thank the tree spirit, bid farewell to the guardians, and pull up Circle. On each full moon and Sabbat, place your hands on the tree talisman, and reaffirm its protective energy by saying,

"Blessed be this divine tree.
Please protect my home and stand strong,
Please bless my home and stand long,
By the dryad of the tree, blessed be!"

Gardening With Flower Essences

Gardening is a sure way to connect with the flower faeries. We are fortunate to live on a planet with thousands of flowers. Each flower has a faery connected with it, and also has an outward sign or signature that shows its true nature and specific use. For example, the milky juice of milkweed is its signature, so the plant is used to ensure the flow of milk in nursing mothers. One way to connect with the flower faeries is to take Bach flower essences just before you go outside to garden. Flower essences are powerful and effective potions for communing with the faeries.

* Bach flower essences.

* Your garden or yard.

* Your Faery Magick journal and pen.

1. Go outside and begin walking around your yard. What are the first three living flowers you notice? Make a mental note of them.

2. Now, select one of the three flowers. Go to a health food store or the Internet, and purchase the Bach flower essence that corresponds to the flower. If you can't find a matching essence, then select one of the other flowers of the original three.

3. Go outside in the morning or early afternoon with the Bach flower essence and your journal and pen, and sit or stand next to the corresponding flower. Take the essence (Following the container directions, put a few drops under your tongue).

4. Now, focus your awareness on the flower. Place your hands on the flower, and take a deep and complete breath in and out. Feel the qualities of the flower and its fae. Feel the flower's essence in your heart. Think about how you and the flower faery are alike, and become one with the essence of the flower. Speak to the flower faery within the flower. Ask the fae how you can make your home safe, happy, healthy, and prosperous. Make a note of the date, and then jot down the answers you receive in your journal. Do this for at least 30 minutes.

5. Repeat this process for at least 28 days (an entire moon cycle), for the best results. This will match your personal energies to the faery energies. By aligning your energies, it is much easier to see, sense, and communicate with the flower faeries.

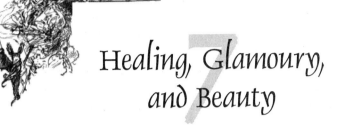

Healing, Glamoury, and Beauty

Once at midnight in early spring, a man who was hump-backed was walking home and he met the faeries merrily singing and dancing. He courteously danced with the faery queen and he sang a song with them, "Monday, Tuesday, Wednesday." He did it so well that the faeries removed his hump. The man happily returned home as a handsome and straight-bodied man. He kept quiet about his secret meeting with the faeries even though many of his neighbors asked him how he lost his hump. As a reward for his courtesy and discretion, he married a fine woman, had many strong sons and beautiful daughters, and lived a long and happy life.

Shortly after the meeting between the hump-backed man and the faeries, a dour and boisterous tailor walked past the exact same spot, and he was also invited by the faeries to join their singing and dancing. The tailor caught the faery queen by the waist when he danced with her, and she resented his familiarity. As he joined in their singing, he added, "Thursday" to the faery song and ruined it. As a reward for his rudeness and ill manners, the faeries took the hump they had removed from the hump-backed man *and clapped it upon the tailor's back, and there it remained. The conceited and dour fellow went home a hump-back. He was ridiculed by his neighbors, and lived a short life of misery and agony until he died.*

As shown in the previous story, "Benbecula," in the Western Herbrides in Scotland, keeping your promises, being gracious, truthful, and honest are virtues respected and rewarded by the fae. Faeries also help mortals who keep their secrets and guard against intrusions upon their privacy. Polite manners, gentle words, and a true heart are assets when communing with the faeries. Your ability to share, be open, and generous are appreciated, while bragging, being conceited, greedy, and boastful are unpopular.

Faeries as Spirits of Nature, have the Natural powers to help heal and revitalize us and our planet. In order to gain their beneficial powers, you need to energetically (not necessarily physically) merge with the Elemental energies of Earth, Air, Fire, and Water, with directed intention and genuine desire, and without fear. As a guidepost, the Earth faeries welcome cheerful benevolence, truthfulness, and kindness, while the Air faeries welcome loyalty, consistency, and continuity. Cool composure, patience, and calm are required when working with the Fire faeries, and the Water faeries respond best to solid, steady, and benevolent firmness and congruence.

The magickal power of faery glamoury, like their healing power, can be used to help you feel and look more beautiful and energized. Faeries can change their shape, and most everything else's shape at will. They make things appear as they want them to appear. This is glamoury. With their magickal creative license, they can make an acorn look like a magnificent palace, a lady seem like a dragon, an old man seem like a baby, and a penny seem like a roomful of golden coins. They can also use their glamoury to magickally shape a more beautiful you.

More often than not, when you catch sight of a faery, it is in a glamoury form. It is very unlikely that you will ever see a faery being in its true form. If you are fortunate enough to do so, you may only catch sight of the faery out of the corner of your eye, and then lose sight of it at almost the same moment. As we've discussed, many animals, such as cats and dogs, can more easily perceive the faeries than people, and you may notice them staring at what seem to be invisible beings when you are making Faery Magick. I invite you to apply the following healing and beauty spells to access the healing power and magickal glamoury of the helpful fae.

Morning Dew Healing Magick

Attune yourself to the Elements to draw upon the helpful healing powers of the Earth, Air, Fire, and Water faeries. Just before dawn on a warm day, make this healing tea. Then enjoy a walk with the helpful faeries in the healing morning dew. The morning dew, especially on May Day and Midsummer, possesses magickal healing energies.

- Chamomile tea bag.
- 1 cup boiling water.
- 3 fresh mint leaves.
- A slice of lemon.

1. Gather together the ingredients for the tea. Hold the tea bag in your power hand, and empower it by saying:

> *"I empower this healing tea with these herbs."*

Now put the tea bag in the cup of boiling water.

2. Hold the mint leaves in your power hand, and say:

"I empower this healing tea with these mint leaves."

Add the mint leaves to the tea.

3. Hold the slice of lemon in your power hand, and empower it by repeating:

"I empower this healing tea with this lemon."

Squeeze the lemon into the tea, and sip the tea potion. A cup of healing tea on a quiet morning warms and comforts, bringing peaceful joy. As you sip the healing tea, think about the ways you would like to renew and heal yourself.

4. Now, go outdoors and walk barefoot (or wearing cotton socks), through grass or thick ground cover moistened with morning dew. Have fun and let the inner child in you run wild in the wet grass. Walk for at least 10 minutes. As you do, softly chant:

"The dawn brings the dew and healing true
Healing faeries of North, East, South, and West
By your healing powers, may I be blessed."

5. Gather a few wild flowers, grasses, and stones as you walk.

6. Go back indoors. Put what you have gathered on your Faery Magick altar to remind you of your healing walk.

7. Carry one of the stones with you for at least 81 days. Each day reaffirm the stone's fae healing power by holding it in your power hand, and repeating:

"Healing faeries of North, East, South, and West
By your healing powers, may I be blessed."

Lady of the Lake Healing Journey

The faery journey can be used to help renew and revitalize your body, mind, and spirit. For the most powerful healing benefits, repeat this healing journey during the four hinges of the day: dawn, noon, dusk, and midnight. (Please refer to the Faery May Day Journey in Chapter 5 for specific tape-recording tips.)

✴ A milky quartz crystal.

✴ Soft healing music.

1. Begin by finding a spot where you will not be disturbed or distracted for about 30 minutes. Turn on some soft healing music, and then get as comfortable as possible. Remember to remove your glasses, all jewelry, your wristwatch, belt, shoes, and loosen any clothing that may be binding you. Hold the crystal in your receiving hand, and settle even more comfortably into the surface supporting you. Now imagine breathing in pure white light, and breathing out all the tensions you may be feeling. Do this for a few minutes, relaxing more and more.

2. Next, imagine breathing in bright blue light, and breathing out blue light. Do this for a few minutes as you listen to the relaxing music.

3. Now in your mind's eye, imagine a mountain lake, rimmed by pine trees and sharp rocky mountain peaks. The still glassy surface reflects the trees and mountains that rim the azure-colored lake.

You look out over the water, and see a small island that rests in the center of the lake. Gazing across the water, you see a magickal boat coming toward you. As the boat moves closer, you see a beautiful faery lady guiding the craft. She is dressed in gossamer, water-colored, blue-green robes. Her hair is long and flows like water. She shimmers brighter and brighter as she approaches the lake's shore. She beckons you into the boat, and says, "Come with me to the magickal healing island." You thank the lady and step into the boat, and in an instant you are magickally transported to the shore of the island. You step onto the shore, and take a deep breath of clear mountain air. The lovely faery lady smiles and says, "On this island, winter never comes and no one knows any pain or sorrow. This a magickal place of renewal and healing." She leads you down a path lined by large milky white stones that seem to shimmer brighter and brighter as you walk along. The faery lady explains, "Those who have gone before have left light in every stone for us to follow." The path leads to a small hill. The faery lady knocks three times on the hill, and says, "I am coming home, I am coming home, I am coming home." The hill opens up, and reveals an illuminated stairway into the earth. You enter the hill with the faery lady, and come to a magnificent hall. The walls are lined with milky white stones, and the floor seems to be fashioned from one large crystal. The entire hall is filled with Spirit light, a direct light within the Earth, of Spirit living within matter. In the center of the great hall, a beautiful faery queen sits on a jeweled chair. The lake faery leads you over to the queen and presents you to her. The queen tells you that you are welcome in the hall, and she gives you a milky white quartz crystal. She says to you, "Use this stone to renew and heal your body, mind, and spirit." You hold the stone in your receiving hand, and it feels unusually warm.

The faery queen shows you around the magnificent hall. She leads you to a healing chamber with a crystal pentacle inlaid into the floor with milky white crystals all around it. She beckons you to lay back comfortably on soft cushions in the middle of the pentacle. The cushions are soft and inviting and covered with a fabric as fine as spider webs. The faery queens says, "The crystal pentacle around you contains the healing powers of Earth, Air, Fire, Water, and Spirit. As you relax in this healing chamber, merge with the stones at your head, hands, and feet. Become one with them and absorb their healing powers." As you merge with the essence of the stones, you can feel their healing energies begin to fill you completely. Imagine breathing in their healing light, feeling more energized and revitalized. In your mind's eye, you connect the stones in the healing chamber into one, as if weaving them together with a bright white thread. As you do so, the healing light grows stronger and brighter. You breathe the light into every cell of your body, and feel radiant and shining, filled with bright healing energy. Take your time and breathe in plenty of healing light into your body, mind, and spirit.

When you are done breathing in healing light, imagine finding yourself standing once again on the shore line of the lake, looking out over the water toward the island. The glassy surface of the lake and the magickal island shimmer in the sunlight. You look out over the water and take a deep breath of mountain air, feeling refreshed and renewed, alive and filled with healing energy. Breathing in the calm blue of the relaxing water, you feel healthier and more in harmony with yourself and the world than ever before.

4. Now, move your toes and fingers, and slowly open your eyes and come back to the present time and place. Stretch your body like a cat, and take a deep breath in, and exhale completely.

5. Put the milky white crystal on your Faery Magick Altar, and use it each time you take this healing journey.

Poppy and Rose Faery Potion

Poppy seeds promote relaxation, longevity, and good health. In ancient Greece, athletes consumed poppy seeds for added endurance and stamina. Use the natural healing qualities of poppy seeds and the helpful healing powers of the rose faeries to promote better health. This healthy poppy and rose faery potion is tasty and easy to make. It makes four large servings, so the whole family can enjoy its faery healing magick! (Remeber to use caution when ingesting roses, as some may be **poisonous**.)

+ 10 oz. of egg noodles.
+ 2 Tbs. extra-light olive oil.

✴ 1 small, thinly sliced white onion.

✴ 2 finely chopped garlic cloves.

✴ 2 tsp. poppy seeds.

✴ 1 tsp. rose petals.

1. Cook the noodles according to package directions. Then drain the pasta. Put the noodles into a large mixing or pasta bowl, and stir in about half of the olive oil. As you stir the noodles clockwise, say:

> *"May the healing powers of the fae*
> *Fill this potion with magick today."*

2. Put the other half of the olive oil into a pan with the chopped onion. Cook slowly until the onion is very light brown. As you stir the onion clockwise in the pan, repeat:

> *"May the healing powers of the fae*
> *Fill this potion with magick today."*

Take the onion out of the pan with a slotted spoon, and then add it to the noodles. As you stir the onion into the pasta in clockwise circles, repeat:

> *"May the healing powers of the fae*
> *Fill this potion with magick today."*

3. Now, put the garlic into the same oil that you cooked the onions in, and cook it for a minute or two. As you lightly brown the garlic, repeat:

> *"May the healing powers of the fae*
> *Fill this potion with magick today."*

Add the cooked garlic to the pasta. As you stir the garlic into the pasta in clockwise circles, again repeat:

> *"May the healing powers of the fae*
> *Fill this potion with magick today."*

4. Sprinkle the poppy seeds over the pasta, and as you do, repeat:

> *"May the healing powers of the fae*
> *Fill this potion with magick today."*

5. Just before serving, lightly top the healthy potion with the rose petals. As you sprinkle them on top, repeat once again:

> *"May the healing powers of the fae*
> *Fill this potion with magick today."*

As you slowly eat the potion, imagine its faery healing powers filling your body with each and every delicious bite you take.

Dryað Healing Spell

Access the healing powers of the tree dryads by spending time with trees in Nature. The dryads have the power to control storms, make the sun shine, and help the herds and animals multiply and prosper. They have magickal powers of healing, renewal, regeneration, and fertility. Traditionally, passing through a cleft in an oak can help heal and regenerate you. Cast this spell on an afternoon of the full moon or Sabbat for the most powerful healing results.

✴ Sandalwood oil.

✴ A living oak with a cleft in it.

✴ Fresh flowers.

1. In the late afternoon before dusk, go outdoors and find a living oak tree with a cleft in it to sit under. Dusk is one of the four energetic hinges of each day. The door to the Otherworld, to faeryland, swings on these hinges.

2. Draw a Faery Ring around the oak. Then lay the fresh flowers around the Ring.

3. Draw a Faery Magick Circle, and call in the faery guardians.

4. Anoint yourself with the sandalwood oil, and then sit or stand under the tree for a few minutes with your back against the tree trunk.

5. As you relax under the oak, notice the patterns that the changing shadows of the tree leaves cast on your skin and the ground. Feel the tree's essence, and become with the tree and its shadow. Notice how the shadows on the leaves, look like tiny faeries or tree elves flitting to and fro. Look directly at the tree and then at its shadow. Notice the place *in between* the tree and its shadow.

6. Put your hands against the tree itself, and imagine breathing in the strength and natural majesty of the oak tree. Feel its healing strength filling your body as you breathe in its magickal energy.

7. Next, climb through the cleft of the oak three times. Each time you climb through, say:

"Sacred spirit of the tree
Share your healing power with me."

(Note: Go around the tree in a clockwise motion as you move around it to climb back through.)

8. Now, walk around the tree clockwise three times. As you do, chant softly:

"Sacred spirit of the tree
Share your healing power with me."

9. When you are done, thank the tree dryad for her helpful healing energies. Erase the traces of your Faery Ring, thank the faery guardians, and pull up your Faery Magick Circle.

Faery Garden Picnic

Take this summer faery picnic in your backyard under a fruit tree, or in your flower or vegetable garden. Having fun and enjoying life is essential to good health. To add some faery flower healing power to your picnic, make hollyhock sandwiches with poppy seed bread. The genus name of hollyhock is "althaea," which means "that which heals." Other edible flowers include chrysanthemums, geraniums, nasturtiums, pansies, poppies, sunflowers, tulips, and violets.

⁎ 4 slices poppy seed bread.

⁎ 4 hollyhock blossoms.

⁎ 1 thinly sliced tomato.

⁎ 4 thin slices of Monterey Jack cheese.

⁎ 1/2 cup alfalfa sprouts.

⁎ 2 pinches toasted sesame seeds.

⁎ Your favorite salad dressing.

1. Put the slices of bread on plates. Place your hands, palms down, just above the slices of bread, and empower them by saying:

> *"By the power of the flower faeries*
> *Fill this food with healing energy."*

2. Layer the thinly sliced cheese and tomato on top of the bread. As you add the slices, repeat:

> *"By the power of the flower faeries*
> *Fill this food with healing energy."*

3. Next, pile the hollyhock blossoms on. As you do, say:

> *"By the power of the flower faeries*
> *Fill this food with healing energy."*

4. Then top the hollyhock blossoms with sprouts. Say:

> *"By the power of the flower faeries*
> *Fill this food with healing energy."*

5. Spoon on the salad dressing on top, and say:

> *"By the power of the flower faeries*
> *Fill this food with healing energy."*

6. Then sprinkle the open-faced sandwich with toasted sesame seeds, and say:

> *"By the power of the flower faeries*
> *Fill this food with healing energy."*

7. As you eat the hollyhock sandwich, imagine each bite filling you with the powerful healing energy of the flower faeries.

Faery Beauty Dream Bag

Like the old European dream or comfort pillows, this beauty bag imparts the natural beauty of the flower faeries to you while you sleep.

- A mixing bowl.
- 1/2 cup lavender.
- 1/4 cup chamomile.
- 1/2 cup rose petals.
- 1/4 cup verbena.
- A white drawstring bag.

1. Put the lavender, chamomile, rose petals, and verbena into a mixing bowl. Then mix the bits of herbs together with the fingers of your power hand. As you do, say three times:

> *"Faery flowers, come alive*
> *Magickal powers now thrive*
> *Impart your beauty to me*
> *As I dream, so shall it be!"*

2. Tuck the beauty bag into your pillowcase. As you drift to sleep, repeat to yourself:

"Faery flowers impart your beauty to me as I dream."

As you sleep, the movement of your head will crush the herbs together, releasing their magickal powers.

3. In the morning, write down everything you recall about your dreams. Keep the beauty bag in your pillow for the next 28 nights, and continue writing down everything you remember from your dreams. Use your notes to empower yourself and dream a more beautiful you into being.

Faery Skin Glamoury

When you dream about daisies, it brings you good health and good fortune. Also called bruisewort, when crushed, daisy petals are therapeutically beneficial for the skin. As with daisies, roses and aloe have long been used to attain softer and more lovely skin. Use this skin glamoury formula to encourage your Natural beauty to blossom:

* 1/4 cup fresh daisy blossoms.
* 1/2 cup fresh rose petals.
* 2 cups boiling water.
* A ceramic (not metal) pot.
* Aloe vera gel.

1. Pick the flowers at noon. As you pick them, thank the flower faeries for their beautiful blossoms.

2. Put the blossoms in rapidly boiling water, and then turn off the heat, and let the mixture steep for at least 20 minutes.

3. After the flower water has cooled, liberally apply it to your face and neck area. As you do, chant:

"My Natural beauty is blossoming
By the flower fae, blessed be!"

4. Next, apply the aloe vera gel to your face and neck areas. As you do, once again chant:

"My Natural beauty is blossoming
By the flower fae, blessed be!"

5. Stain the flower water and store it in a glass jar in the refrigerator. Use it all within a week of making it, for best results.

Faery Beauty Affirmation

The faery queens are more beautiful than any mortal woman on Earth. For example, Oonagh, wife of Finvarra (the king of the Western faeries), has long, shining golden hair that sweeps the ground. She wears robes of silver gossamer that glitter with dew drops that look like thousands of tiny diamonds. Use the Natural beauty of the faery queens and the butterfly faeries to affirm your inner and outer beauty. Do this spell at dusk on a Friday, close to, or on a full moon, for the best results:

* Soft music.

* Fresh roses.

* A white candle.

* A ballpoint pen.

* Rose oil.

* A picture of a butterfly.

1. Turn on some soft music, and then draw a Faery Magick Ring. Sprinkle it with fresh rose petals. Then draw a Faery Magic Circle and call in the faery guardians.

2. Use the ballpoint pen to write your initials on the candle body. Then write the word *"Beautiful"* on top of your

initials. Dress the candle with a thin film of rose oil, and place the candle in its holder on the altar.

3. Anoint yourself with the rose oil.

4. Now, put the picture of the butterfly in front of the candle, where you can easily see it, and wipe the oil from your hands.

5. Light the candle, dedicating it to the beautiful faery queens and the butterfly faeries. Then say three times:

"By the blessings of the winged fae, each day I feel more beautiful in every way."

6. Focus your awareness on the picture of the butterfly for a few minutes. Then close your eyes. In your mind's eye, imagine a circle of beautiful butterfly faeries. Now, imagine a second circle of butterfly faeries flying around the first circle. Then imagine a third circle of gossamer-winged butterfly faeries forming around the second circle. Imagine standing in the very center of the three butterfly Faery Circles. As you stand there, you can feel their Natural healing energy flowing into your body, mind, and spirit. Their wings softly brush against your skin and the sensation is delightfully magickal. Your entire being is filled with radiant winged power and beauty. In the presence of these gorgeous and exquisite butterfly faeries, you feel as if you, too, could fly freely through the air. In this elevated state of being, you are filled with a magickal sense of beauty and harmony. Stay in the center of the butterfly Faery Circle for several minutes.

7. Thank the faery queens and butterfly faeries. Bid farewell to the faery guardians, and pull up the Faery Magick Circle.

8. Write the beauty affirmation on a sheet of paper or index card, and tape it somewhere you will see it every day. Repeat the affirmation out loud at least three times a day for 28 days:

*"By the blessings of the winged fae, each day I feel more
beautiful in every way."*

9. Be sure to plant butterfly attracting flowers, such as
asters, goldenrods, phlox, coneflowers, catmints, yarrow, milkweed, California dutchman's-pipevine, dianthus, cinquefoil,
butterflyweed, and butterfly bush, in your garden and around
your home to attract more Natural butterfly and flower
faery beauty power into your life each and every day. By
keeping your soil healthy and gardening organically, you
can produce more vibrant flowers and foods. By communing with the faeries, you can learn the best plants to grow
in specific locations to create the most harmony and beauty.

Faery Glamoury Bath

Take this bath on a full moon or on the eight sabbats
just before doing magick, going on a romantic date, or
going out on the town. It will relax and fill your body,
mind, and spirit with Faery Magick and Beauty.

* A comb.
* Two sheets of beeswax.
* A wick.
* Lavender oil.
* Pennyroyal oil.
* Rose oil.
* A working tub.
* Your favorite moisturizer.

1. Lay the two sheets of beeswax out flat. (Note: You can
purchase beeswax sheets from bee supply houses, craft stores, and
over the Internet.) Apply nine drops each of lavender, pennyroyal,
and rose oil on each of the sheets. Rub the oil over the sheets, and
then place the sheets together. Put the wick on the edge of the top

sheet, and then roll the sheets tightly over the wick into a candle. Hold the candle in your hands, and empower it by saying:

"Beautiful faeries of Earth, Air, Fire, and Sea
Please bless me with your Natural grace and beauty."

2. Next, run a warm bath. Add three drops of rose oil into the bath water. As you do this, repeat:

"Beautiful faeries of Earth, Air, Fire, and Sea
Please bless me with your Natural grace and beauty."

3. Put the candle in a place where you can see it while bathing. Before you get into the tub, light the candle, dedicating it to the faeries of Earth, Air, Fire, and Water.

4. Now, get into the tub and gaze at the candlelight. Turn your awareness to your best features, and imagine them being even more magickally attractive. See yourself as beautiful and joyful. Allow the scent of the oil to fill your senses as you soak in the warm water.

5. Soak for a while, imagine being beautiful within and without, and then get out of the tub and dry off.

6. Liberally apply your favorite moisturizer. As you do, repeat:

"Beautiful faeries of Earth, Air, Fire, and Sea
Please bless me with your Natural grace and beauty."

Anoint yourself with the lavender oil, repeating:

"Beautiful faeries of Earth, Air, Fire, and Sea
Please bless me with your Natural grace and beauty."

7. Then use the comb to slowly comb your hair. As you do, chant:

"One, two, three, bless me with fae beauty."

You are now ready for a night of magickal beauty.

Prosperity and Wealth

Once upon a time, there was a poor and lonely boy, who drive his cart filled with turf back and forth every day, and made a little money by selling the turf. Strange, moody, mostly silent, and rarely speaking to anyone, the boy was an outcast in his village. The people in the village said that he was a faery changeling. He spent his nights reading old bits of books he had picked up here and there. From his readings, the one thing the boy wished and longed for above all else was to give up the dreary turf cart and be wealthy and rich. He wanted to live in peace and harmony in a beautiful house with magnificent gardens, with nothing but books around him.

In the books he read, he learned that the leprechauns were magickal beings who knew the secret places where gold was hidden. Day by day, the boy watched for the little cobbler leprechaun who sat under a nearby hedge and mended shoes. Day by day, he listened for the sharp click, clack, click, clack, of the leprechaun's magickal hammer.

One evening, just as the sun was setting, the boy spotted the little leprechaun under a dock leaf working away with a tiny hammer. Dressed in green, with his hat cocked sideways, the little fellow was taken completely unaware as the boy jumped down from where he was hiding in his turf cart, and grabbed the leprechaun firmly by the neck.

The boy cried, "Now, I've got you and I won't let you go until you tell me where to find the hidden gold."

"Easy now, don't hurt me, and I will tell you where it is hidden," replied the leprechaun. "But mind you, I could hurt you if I chose to, for I have the power to do so, but I won't because we are related, you and I. We are cousins once removed. As we are related, I'll be good and show you the secret hiding place of the gold, treasure that only those with faery blood such as yourself can have and keep. Come with me to the old faery fort called Lipenshaw–for that is where it is hidden. But come quickly, for when the last red glow of the sun vanishes, the gold will also disappear, and you will never find it again."

"Let's go then," said the boy, and he carried the little fellow into the turf cart, and drove off. In an instant, they were at the old fort. They entered through a secret door fashioned into the stone wall.

While passing through the doorway, the leprechaun said to the boy, "Look around you."

The entire floor of the fort was covered with gold pieces, and there were silver vessels lying about in such plenty that all the riches of the world seemed to be gathered together in this one secret place.

"Now take what you want," said the leprechaun, "but hurry up and make haste, for if the stone door shuts you will be trapped here and will never leave this place."

So the boy gathered up the gold and silver into his arms and quickly flung it into his cart, and dashed out the door. He was on his way back for more when the door shut with a thunder-like clap. The place became dark as the grave, and the boy never saw the little leprechaun again.

The boy drove home with his faery treasure, and counted his riches. There were enough bright yellow-gold pieces for a queen's ransom. He carefully hid the treasure away in his turf cart, told no one of his adventures, and went to sleep.

The very next morning, the boy took his riches and went to Dublin. He put all of his gold and silver into the bank. He discovered that he was now indeed as wealthy as the rich Lords he had read about in the old books.

With his new wealth, the boy ordered a fine house to be built with magnificent gardens. He had carriages and servants and hundreds of books to his heart's content. He gathered all the wise men around and asked them to teach him how to be a gentleman. Over the years, he became a great and powerful man in his country, where his memory is still held in high honor, and his descendants are living to this day, still rich and prosperous. Favorites of the faeries, the family's wealth has never decreased. They have given generously to the poor and are known for their friendly heart and their liberal hand.

The riches of the faeries and their magickal gifts have been a mainstay in faery tales. This story, adapted from *Leprechaun Companion*, by Niall MacNamara, has been passed down for generations, and shows that with a little ingenuity and wisdom, the silver and gold riches of the faeries are within mortal grasp, yesterday, today, and always.

The first step toward gaining faery riches is to *think wealthy.* Prosperity is a personal asset that begins in your mind. You need to develop a wealthy mind set. Think prosperous, and perceive the world as a place of overflowing abundance. As you turn your mind to prosperity and move toward your goals, you will begin to work smarter by increasing your abilities, and eventually reap the abundant harvest of your efforts.

Magick adds the divine component to your prosperity goals. To be prosperous, turn your mind toward your financial aspirations as much as you can, especially when doing magick. The fear of failure lies within all of us. Faery Magick can help you move passed that fear and go after what it is you want in life. Through intention, expectation, deep desire, and merging with the faeries and the power of the Elements, you can direct an immense amount of Divine Power toward your goals. Instead of doing it all on your own, the faeries, Elemental powers, magickal beings, and the goddesses and gods are there to help, guide, and protect you.

The most important thing to keep in mind when dealing with the faeries is to take nothing for granted. The best way to gain their gifts and favors is by treating them with total respect. Graciously accept what you are given with a friendly heart. You need to have a true heart whenever you interact with the faeries as they can see through your every deception. Greed, avarice, exploitation, and corruption have no place in Faery Magick, or for that matter, in your daily life.

Faery Gold Charm Box

Many a faery tale describes faery palaces lavishly decorated with silver and gold. Even faery horses wear shoes of silver and bridles of gold. Faeries are well known for their magickal gifts of gold, gossamer fabric, and pots filled with food and grain that continuously replenish themselves. For example, the industrious and merry leprechauns know where to find hidden treasure, and if they like you, they will lead you to the place where the pot of gold lies buried. Draw the gold and silver treasure of the faeries into your life and find your own hidden treasure with this charm. Make it on a Wednesday at the beginning of the year, just before sunset, on or close to a full moon:

* Smudge stick.
* 7 pinches of rosemary.
* A small golden-colored or brass box.
* A sheet of paper and pen.

* A silver coin.
* A white stone from Nature.
* 7 pinches vervain.
* 7 pinches poppy seeds.

1. Draw a Faery Ring, and scatter the rosemary clockwise around the Ring. Then draw a Faery Magick Circle, and call in the faery guardians.

2. Light the smudge stick, and pass the other items through the smoke to energetically clear them of any unwanted energies. Extinguish the smudge completely when you are done.

3. Next, use the pen to write down the exact amount of silver and gold (the amount of money) you want to draw into your life this year. Write down how you are going to receive the money. Some example are: through your regular job; overtime; opening your own business; selling personal items or real estate; writing a song, cookbook or a software program, craft-making; playing the stock market; or from a family trust.

4. Out loud, read the amount of money and how you are going to get it, three times.

5. Put the sheet of paper on a flat surface, and put the coin, stone, vervain, and poppy seeds in the center of the paper. Fold the paper once, then again, and then a third time, folding the contents up as you do so.

6. Carefully place the folded paper and contents into the gold box. Close the box, and hold it in your hands. Empower it by saying:

"Faery gold and prosperity
Newfound fortune and money
Continuously flow to me
As I will, so shall it be!"

7. Continue holding the box in your hands as you imagine having the exact amount of money that you want this year. Imagine how that money is coming into your life. Imagine the action steps you can take, and all the ways that money and treasure will flow into your life, from your honest efforts, golden opportunities, and truly bright ideas.

8. When you are done, thank the faeries, bid farewell to the guardians, and pull up your Faery Magick Circle.

9. Put the charm box in a place of honor where you will see it every day. Once a day, empower the fortunate power of your faery gold charm box by holding the box in your hands, and saying:

> *"Faery gold and prosperity*
> *Newfound fortune and money*
> *Continuously flow to me*
> *As I will, so shall it be!"*

Faery Mound Magick

Some say that parts of Ireland are more thickly populated with faeries than with people. Ireland abounds with places having Faery associations such as the "Sheegys," the faery hill in Donegal and "Sheeauns," the faery mounds. You, too, can use the higher vantage point of a the faery mound or hilltop to draw prosperity and wealth into your life. Do this spell on a spring morning before the last spring rain:

✳ A quartz crystal.

✳ Fresh flowers.

✳ A package of sunflower seeds.

✳ An orange.

1. Gather the items together, and go to a hilltop, mound, canyon ridge, or mountain just after dawn where you are high above the ordinary world.

2. Use the fresh flowers to make a Faery Ring, and then sprinkle the sunflower seeds clockwise, on the inside of the Faery Ring. Draw a Faery Magick Circle of light on top of the other two circles, and call in the faery guardians.

3. Sit down in the center of the triple Circle, facing East, and merge with the energy of the sun for a few minutes.

4. Next, hold the crystal in your power hand, and let it warm. Then hold it upward toward the sun and say:

"May the divine power of the sun fill this stone."

5. Imagine the warmth and powerful light of the sun filling the stone in your hand for a few minutes. Now say three times:

"I offer this stone in heartfelt friendship to the faeries."

6. Put the stone in a secret hiding place on the hilltop or mound, for instance, in the nook of a tree, or under a bush or rock, as a heartfelt gift to the faeries.

7. Go back and sit in the center of your Faery Ring. Peel the orange, and enjoy the sweet fruit as you take in the view around you. As you eat the orange slices, imagine your life being more and more prosperous. Imagine drawing riches into your life each and every day.

8. When you are done, bid farewell to the faery guardians, and pull up the Circle.

9. Use the heel of your power foot (right foot if you are right-footed), to gently push the sunflower seeds into the ground so the seeds can take root and grow after the next rain.

Springtime Offering

The Blajini, also called the "Kindly Ones," live on the banks of rivers, creeks, and streams. When they find your offerings of eggshells, basil, and flowers, they will bestow their fortunate gifts upon you. Do this faery offering on a Monday in the springtime:

* The eggshells of seven eggs.
* 7 pinches of basil.
* A package of wildflowers.

1. Put the eggshells and pinches of basil together in a cup. Take the filled cup and the seeds, and go to a river, stream, or creek with running water.

2. Sit comfortably next to the water, and run your hands slowly through it. Take a deep breath in, and smell the dampness in the air next to the water. Look into the water, and notice how the current flows and how the water laps at the banks as it moves. Merge with the Water, and become one with it. As you do this, say:

"Kindly Ones, I bring you springtime offerings.
May you thrive and prosper. Blessed be!"

3. Now, softly toss the mixture of eggshells and basil in the cup into the water a pinch at a time. As you do this, chant:

"Kindly Ones, may you thrive and prosper. Blessed be!"

4. Draw a small Faery Ring next to the river, creek, or stream bank with the heel of your shoe, a stick, or pointed rock. Open the seed package, and carefully pour the seeds into your receiving hand. Now cup your power hand over the seeds, and empower them by saying:

"Kindly Ones, I pray you
Generously empower these seeds
With your gifts of prosperity."

5. Plant the wildflower seeds in the Faery Ring. Sprinkle them clockwise around the ring, and then lightly cover them with soil. When you are done covering the seeds, say"

> *"May every seed I plant grow fruitful*
> *Blessed and protected by the Kindly Ones*
> *May my fortune grow strong and blossom*
> *With gifts from the helpful Kindly Ones,*
> *By the powers of the faeries, blessed be!"*

6. Dip the empty cup in the water, and gently pour the water over the planted seeds. Water the surface thoroughly, and then say"

> *"May every seed I water grow fruitful*
> *Blessed and protected by the Kindly Ones.*
> *May my fortune grow strong and blossom*
> *With gifts from the helpful Kindly Ones.*
> *By the powers of the faeries, blessed be!"*

7. When you are done, thank the Kindly Ones, bid farewell to the faery guardians, and pull up the Circle. Your offering is complete.

Faery Shapeshifting Spell

Akin to the Swan Maiden in folklore, the Selkies of Ireland are probably the most ancient shapeshifters of all. Popularized by the acclaimed film *The Secret of Roan Ish*, a Selkie is a magickal being who can slip out of her seal skin and become human-like. A Selkie sheds her skin, becomes human-like, marries a mortal, and has children. At some point in time, the Selkie slips back into her seal skin and disappears into the sea forever.

This magickal spell shows you how to slip into your magickal skin and become one with the faeries to draw more prosperity into your life. Do this work outdoors at dawn or just before dusk in a private and quiet spot in Nature on a Sabbat, full or waxing moon. Make sure you won't be disturbed for about 30 minutes.

 * A quartz crystal.

 * Fresh flowers.

1. Draw a Faery Ring, and sprinkle the flowers around its outline. Then draw the Faery Magick Circle, and call in the faery guardians.

2. Hold the crystal in your receiving hand (left hand if your are right-handed). Close your eyes, and take a deep, relaxing breath in, hold it for three counts, and then breathe out any tensions you may be feeling. Now, take another deep breath. As you do, imagine breathing in bright white light into your body, hold your breath for three counts, and then breathe out any residual tension. Breathe in the bright white light once again, let go of any stress you may be feeling as you exhale. Take another deep breath in, and imagine breathing bright golden light into your body. Take another deep and relaxing breath in and out, while imagining breathing the bright golden light of the sun into your entire being.

3. Take a wonderfully relaxing golden breath, and imagine yourself effortlessly slipping into the crystal in your hand. First, imagine the tips of your toes entering the stone, then your feet and ankles, followed by your calves, knees, thighs, hips, stomach, back, arms, shoulders, neck, and head. You slip completely into the crystal, into the lattice of the stone. Merge with the stone and become one with it. (Note: If you have any problems doing this, go ahead and suspend your belief for a few minutes, and just pretend you are energetically slipping into the stone. With practice, you will find it easier and easier to shift your awareness and become one with the stone.)

4. Now, with your eyes still closed, imagine a faery being standing front of you. Ask the faery her or his name. If you don't receive a name, end the spell, and start over again until you do get a name. Be sure to remember the faery's name.

5. Respectfully observe the faery from every angle. See and sense the faery being. Merge with the faery being, and be one with her or him. Imagine energetically melding with the faery. Begin with the tips of your toes, then your feet and ankles, as well as your calves, knees, thighs, hips, stomach, back, arms, shoulders, neck, and head, slipping totally into the faery being and becoming one with her or him.

6. While you are one with the faery, with your mind, ask her or him:

"Please show me the ways I can draw more prosperity and abundance into my life."

Take a deep breath, and focus on your question.

7. Wait for a reply. Remember the answer you receive. If you don't receive an immediate answer, ask your question a total of three times, and wait for the reply.

8. Now, rub the stone between your fingers, and slowly open your eyes. Move your hands and feet, and stretch your body to bring your awareness back to the present time and space. Clap your hands three times to center yourself.

9. Write down the name of the faery and the answers you received in your Faery Magick journal. Also, make a note of how you felt before and after the shapeshifting experience. Keep your shapeshifting crystal on your Faery Magick altar so you can frequently repeat this spell to draw more faery abundance and riches to you.

Hollyhock Faery Power

Each and every flower has a flower faery spirit within it. From inside each flower, from the flower faery, comes a voice and a scent. Sometimes the voice is quiet, sometimes loud. Often the scent is fragrant, while other times it's hardly noticeable. Just as anyone can tell a person by their voice and scent, every flower and its faery spirit can be identified by its voice and scent. You don't have to be psychic to hear the faery voice. Just take some time to sit quietly by the flower and smell it and listen.

Hollyhock flower faeries have a strong voice and very little fragrance. Greatly favored by the faeries, the regal and stately hollyhock blossoms attract good luck and fortune. It is customary to grow hollyhocks around your house to attract money, success, and material wealth of all kinds.

✳ A package of hollyhock flower seeds.

1. Take the package of seeds and go outside your home.

2. Hold the package of seeds in between your hands, and empower them by saying:

"I empower these seeds with faery wealth and riches."

3. Now, plant the hollyhock seeds around your home according to the package instructions. As you do this say:

"I plant these seeds in honor of the faeries
May they grow strong, high, and beautiful.
Hear me now, beautiful and generous Hollyhock faeries
May my good luck, fortune, and joy grow with these flowers.
By the powers of the garden faeries, blessed be!"

4. Water the seeds regularly. As the hollyhocks grow and blossom year after year, so too will your good luck, fortune, and joy. (Note: You can also put hollyhock blossoms in salads and sandwiches to add faery power to them. They have a delicate taste much like mild green onions.)

Faery Prosperity Wand

Many a tale tells of the magick wands of the faeries: wands that change people into animals, wands that heal, and wands that turn coal into gold. Wands are the most ancient of magickal tools, used to open the doorway into magickal realms. They are usually made from the wood of a fruit tree, and thus contain the spirit of the tree. Because of this, wands can be used to command power over the Elements and influence energy in specific patterns.

* A cup of milk.

* 3 pieces of bread.

* A 16-inch long apple tree branch.

* Non-toxic gold paint and paintbrush.

* Newspaper.

* 8 small gold-colored or silver-colored bells.

* Gold and silver embroidery thread.

* 8 small gold and silver silk flowers.

* Silver and gold beads.

1. During a waxing moon cycle in the spring or summer, take the milk and bread, and go outside and find an apple tree to cut your wand from. If you can't find an apple tree, a peach, pear, or plum tree will also work.

2. Set the cup of milk and bread next to the tree trunk, and then take a few minutes to center your awareness. Take a deep breath, and breathe in the energy of the tree. Do this at least three times.

3. Now, slowly walk around the tree three times clockwise. As you do, praise the tree spirit by chanting:

"Beautiful dryad, magnificent tree, blessed be."

4. Place both palms on the tree or lean against it, and become one with the tree spirit. Communicate with the faery dryad, and

ask if you may have a branch. You will receive a feeling of yes or no. If yes, proceed. If no, find another tree and try again.

5. Use a nearby stick or rock to dig a small hole in the ground at the base of the tree. Pour the milk into the hole and put the bread on top as an offering to the tree dryad. Do not cover the offering. Thank the dryad by saying:

> *"Spirit dryad, I thank you*
> *For giving me a branch of your body.*
> *Send your divine power into it*
> *By Earth, Air, Fire, and Sea*
> *Spirit dryad, blessed be!"*

6. Snap off the branch or cut it with a small saw. Take the appropriate safety precautions as you proceed.

7. Next, take the branch home, put the newspapers down, and paint it gold. Once it is painted, let the wand dry. Put it outside in a safe place or on a window sill to cure for an entire moon cycle of 28 days. This charges it with sun and moon energy.

8. Tie the bells on the wand with the thread. With each bell you tie on, say:

> *"Prosperity and wealth come my way.*
> *So be it, forever and a day."*

9. Tie the flowers on the wand with the thread. With each flower you fasten on the wand, say:

> *"My wealth is blossoming in every way*
> *So be it, forever and a day."*

10. Fasten the gold and silver beads to the ends of the thread. As you knot the ends, repeat:

> *"Prosperity and wealth come my way.*
> *So be it, forever and a day."*

11. Empower you wand by holding it upward between your hands, and saying:

> *"With this wand of the fae*
> *Prosperity and wealth come my way*
> *So be it, forever and a day."*

12. Use your wand every day to bring you more and more prosperity and wealth. Just before planning your next action step in business, before signing contracts, closing business deals, or before going to work, hold the wand upward in your power hand, shake it three times, and repeat with clear intention and a true heart:

> *"With this wand of the fae*
> *Prosperity and wealth now come my way*
> *From North, East, South, and West*
> *By Spirit, Earth, Air, Fire, and Sea*
> *Now grant me golden opportunities and prosperity*
> *By the power of the faeries, blessed be!"*

Elf Abundance Spell

Today, elves are Santa Claus's little helpers, but in ancient Norse mythology, the white, light elves are divine helpers with supernatural powers. Found in secluded and untouched forests and woods, the white, light elves are gentle and kind, with no ill will or avarice. They are thin, quick, and light as the air itself. Amazingly strong, standing between 5 ft. and 7 ft. tall, elves have green, blue, silver, or gold cat-like eyes and sometimes have cat-like ears.

The white, light elves live in Alfheim, the land between Asgard (the home of the gods) and Midgard (the middle world of mortals). Frey, the sun god, is the lord of Alfheim. The elves can enter Midgard at any time they desire to help mortals. Beware, as they will only befriend you if you firmly live by your own code. Paul Anka's song "My Way" depicts this concept. This Elf Abundance Spell can help you set and attain your prosperity goals. For best results, do it at sunset on the evening of the new moon.

* A silver candle.

* Sage incense.

* A piece of moonstone.

* A silver coin.

* Two sheets of paper and a pen.

* Fresh flowers.

1. Set up your Faery Magick altar indoors. Draw a Faery Magick Ring, scattering the fresh flowers clockwise around it. Then draw your Faery Magick Circle, and call in the faery guardians.

2. Light the candle, dedicating it to the Fire faeries. Light the sage incense, dedicating it to the winged, Air faeries. Carefully pass the stone and coin through the smoke to clear them of unwanted energies, and set them on back on the altar.

3. Next, use the pen to write the "S" Sowilo Rune on the top of each sheet of paper, on the front and back sides of both. Sowilo symbolize the sun, and is associated with the world of the white, light elves of Alfheim.

4. Now write down your three main prosperity goals on the sheet of paper. Number them, 1, 2, and 3. For example, you might write:

1. *Start my own business this year.*

2. *Save $10,000 this year.*

3. *Get a promotion and salary increase this month.*

Draw five-pointed stars all the way around your writing in a clockwise circle. Turn the paper over and write down one step you can take to attain each of the prosperity goals you wrote down on the other side. (Also number them 1, 2, and 3.) Draw stars clockwise around the action steps. Repeat this process on the second sheet of paper, so the two sheets are identical.

5. Place one of the sheets on the altar, the "goals side" facing up. Put the coin in the middle of the paper and the moonstone on the coin. Fold the paper three times. Seal the paper with the wax from the candle, being careful not to burn yourself or drip wax on anyone or anything.

6. Now hold the charm in your hands, and empower it by saying:

"White, light elves of the sun
With this offering of stone and silver
I ask for your help in attaining my prosperity goals
By the generous powers of the light elves, blessed be!"

7. As you continue holding the folded paper with the coin and moonstone, imagine the things that can help you attain your goals. Discover the things that can and will influence your life in the future. Imagine some of the people and events that can assist you in making your life more prosperous. Focus on those people, events, and things. Direct your energy toward those empowering thoughts, actions, people, and events, which will move you closer to your goals. Know that you are drawing riches into your life each and every day. Actively seek out the details of your goals, the steps, and helpful people, and see the positive results. Be thorough. Make sure it's what you really want, that it fits you. Go into the changing room in your mind's eye, and try on your prosperity goals. Imagine how your life will change for the better as you attain your goals. Step into the future and be there, doing the magickal works, communing with the elves, drawing those golden opportunities to you, thinking those prosperous thoughts, and taking those necessary action steps to successfully attain your prosperity goals.

8. Now, take the sealed paper, stone, and coin, go outside and bury it under a tree, as an offering to the white, light elves of the sun. Cover it, and draw the Sowilo Rune on top with the index finger of your power hand on the ground where you buried the paper.

9. Go back indoors, bid farewell to the faery guardians, thank the white, light elves of Alfheim, and pull up the Circle. Keep the other sheet of paper on your Faery Magick altar, and reread your prosperity goals and actions steps aloud each morning when you wake up and each night just before you go to sleep for at least 28 days and nights.

Prosperity String Magick

The Norse Mother Goddess Frigga spins the raw material from the abyss into thread that the three Fates, also called the Norns, then weave into the web of life. The Fate Urd takes the thread, Verdandi weaves it into reality, and then Skuld rips it apart and tosses it back into the abyss. Weaving and tying threads is an ancient magickal tradition called String Magick. Do this String magick work at dawn or just before dusk on a full moon to weave more money and wealth into your life.

     ✳ A white 16-inch string.

     ✳ A red 16-inch string.

     ✳ A black 16-inch string.

1. Take the string outdoors and draw a Faery Magick Ring and Circle. Call in the faery guardians.

2. Sit down, and focus your awareness by taking a few deep and complete breaths in and out.

3. Hold the strings in your hands. Take a few minutes to get a clear and strong image of your most cherished prosperity wish. It needs to be something you really want with all of your being: body, mind, and spirit.

4. With your prosperity wish firmly planted in your mind, knot the ends of the string together on both ends. Then loop and slide the strings in and out of your fingers

like a cat's cradle. Use both hands and cradle the threads in your hands as you weave your fingers in and out.

5. As you are weaving the string in and out, turn your mind to your most cherished prosperity wish. Imagine it already coming true. The sound of your voice, the touch of your fingers and hands, and the motion of the strings, all help to empower your wish. They form a link with the energy of your magickal intention and wish. Imagine your wish, the string, your hands, and the movement of your fingers becoming one. Everything is connected and joined into one. Keep weaving your wish into the string for a couple of minutes, and then say:

> *"Faery, Feri, Fata, Fae*
> *Fehu, Fehu, Fehu*
> *Fu, fa, fi, fe, fo, fae*
> *Grant me abundance and prosperity.*
> *Faery, Feri, Fata, Fae*
> *Fehu, Fehu, Fehu*
> *Fa, fi, fe, fo, fu, fae*
> *Grant me fortune and money.*
> *Faery, Feri, Fata, Fae*
> *Fehu, Fehu, Fehu*
> *Fi, fe, fo, fu, fa, fae*
> *From North, East, West, and South*
> *Bring me fortune and prosperity.*
> *By the faeries, blessed be!"*

6. Next, slowly knot the string a total of 16 times, one knot at a time. As you knot the string, imagine actually tying your prosperity wish into the string itself. After you have tied all 16 knots into the string, repeat:

> *"Faery, Feri, Fata, Fae*
> *Fehu, Fehu, Fehu*
> *Fu, fa, fi, fe, fo, fae*
> *Grant me abundance and prosperity.*

Faery, Feri, Fata, Fae
Fehu, Fehu, Fehu
Fa, fi, fe, fo, fu, fae
Grant me fortune and money.
Faery, Feri, Fata, Fae
Fehu, Fehu, Fehu
Fi, fe, fo, fu, fa, fae
From North, East, West, and South
Bring me fortune and prosperity.
By the faeries, blessed be!"

7. When you are done, thank the fates and faeries, bid farewell to the faery guardians, and pull up your Circle. Tie the string on your front door or your business or home to bring more faery fortune and prosperity into your life.

Holiday Treasure Bowl

In Sweden, Jultomte (Santa Claus) is a small and thin leprechaun-like man. The "Little Man" can be either troublesome or benevolent, depending on how well he is treated. Over the years, the Jultomte has become a generous spirit who gives out gifts rather than receives them. Treat the Swedish "Little Man" well by making this Holiday Treasure Bowl for him and he will bestow his magickal gifts upon you and your family. Enjoy the treasure bowl's Natural beauty as a centerpiece on your dining room or kitchen table for several weeks. When the holidays are over, return the bowl's contents to the Earth to bring magickal riches to you the whole year through.

* A large wooden bowl.

* 8 pinecones.

* 2 pomegranates.

* 8 orange rinds.

* 1/2 cup juniper berries.
* 1 cup dried rosebuds.
* 1 cup cedar or pine tips.
* 16 drops rose-scented oil.
* 8 drops pine-scented oil.
* 2 green ribbons.
* 2 red ribbons.
* 2 gold ribbons.
* 2 silver ribbons.
* 8 golden-colored bells.

1. Arrange the pinecones, pomegranates, and orange rinds in the bowl, and then add the berries and rosebuds. Put the cedar or pine tips here and there to add a little greenery to the arrangement. As you put the items into the bowl, chant:

"I offer this treasure bowl to the Little Man. Blessed be!"

2. Slowly add the drops of oil. As you do, repeat:

"I offer this treasure bowl to the Little Man. Blessed be!"

3. Tie a bell on each of the ribbons, and then tie the ribbons into bows and put them in the bowl. With each ribbon and bell you place in the bowl, say:

> *"Treasure bowl of the faeries*
> *Dear Little Man of generosity*
> *Bring me abundance and prosperity*
> *So be it! Blessed be!"*

4. After the holidays, go outside and spread the contents of the treasure bowl (except the ribbons and bells) over the ground.

5. Keep the ribbons and bells on your altar to bring good fortune and magickal gifts to you the whole year round.

Empowerment

Once upon a time, a widower took a second wife. She was a proud woman who was widowed with two daughters, just as proud as herself. Her husband had one daughter named Cinderella, who was gentle, kind, and good, very much like her own mother had been.

The new wife hated the stepdaughter because Cinderella's sweet temper and gentle ways that reflected in her beautiful face, made the frowning faces and ill manners of her own daughters appear even more disagreeable and ugly. So the new wife made Cinderella do all the hardest work of the house. She swept, baked, and washed for the entire household. She wore shabby clothes and slept on a bare garret in the kitchen near the hearth.

It happened that the king's son decided to give a grand ball, and invite all the people of fashion. There was to be dancing two nights in a row, and the food and entertainment were to be the most splendid kind. Cinderella's stepsisters were invited, and they were proud and happy as they talked of the fancy dresses, feathers, and jewels, they were going to wear, as well as the grand people they would surely meet at the palace.

When the great day of the ball came, Cinderella was busy the whole day through helping her step-sisters to get ready. She laced their gowns, combed and braided their hair, arranged their jewels and feathers, and helped them on with their silken slippers. As she helped them dress, they teased and goaded her to amuse themselves. When they were ready, they rode in the family coach to the palace with their mother. Cinderella was left alone. She sat down among the cinders in the hearth and began to sob. Suddenly an old lady with a red cloak, pointed hat, and a magick wand appeared before her. Cinderella was so startled that she stopped crying. The old lady said, "I am your faery Goddess-Mother. I can guess what you wish tonight. You wish to go to the ball at the palace."

Cinderella cried, "Yes, I do, with all of my heart."

The faery Goddess-Mother replied, "Then run into the garden and fetch the largest pumpkin you can find."

Cinderella did as she was told, and ran back to her faery Goddess-Mother with a huge green and yellow pumpkin in her arms.

The faery scooped out the inside of the pumpkin, leaving nothing but the rind. Then she touched it with her faery wand, and at once the pumpkin turned into a fine, golden coach lined with green silk.

The faery then said, "Now fetch the mousetrap."

Cinderella immediately got the mousetrap. In the trap were six mice. The faery Goddess-Mother opened the trap, and as the mice ran out, she touch them with her wand, and they become sleek and prancing white horses. She then said, "These are your coach and horses. Now for the coachman. Bring me the rat trap."

Cinderella quickly brought the rat trap to the faery. There were three rats in it. The faery Goddess-Mother chose the finest of the three rats, and then touched it with her magick wand. At once the rat become a tall, handsome, finely dressed coachman.

The faery then told Cinderella to fetch the six green lizards behind the watering pot. She did so, and the faery touched the lizards with her magick wand. At once they turned into smartly dressed footmen in green uniforms. The coachman mounted the box, and the footmen climbed onto the back of the coach.

"Now your carriage is ready," said the faery Goddess-Mother.

"But how can I go to the ball looking like this?" asked Cinderella, looking down at her shabby clothes.

"You shall soon be more beautiful than your fine coach," her faery Goddess-Mother explained. And with one tap of her magick wand, Cinderella's clothes were transformed into robes of silk and velvet, adorned with colorful feathers, and glittering with jewels. The faery also gave her a pair of shining glass slippers, the prettiest that ever were seen.

"Remember," said the faery, "you must leave the ball before the clock strikes 12 midnight. If you stay any longer, your coach will again become a pumpkin, your horses will become mice, your coachman will turn back into a rat, and your footmen into lizards. And you will find yourself dressed, once more, in shabby clothes."

Cinderella assured her faery Goddess-Mother that she would leave before midnight, and then she entered the coach and rode to the ball in grand style. As she entered the great hall, the musicians stopped playing and the dancers stopped dancing. Everyone gazed in surprise at the beautiful and unknown princess. The prince fell in love at first sight, and rushed immediately to Cinderella's side. All evening he stayed there, dancing every dance with her, and serving her with dainty dishes at supper. Indeed, he was so taken up with her, that he forgot to eat a morsel himself. It was while she was talking to her stepsisters, who didn't know it was Cinderella, that the clock chimed the quarter before twelve. Cinderella rose, and after curtsying to the company, left the palace, and drove home in her coach. She thanked her faery Goddess-Mother for her kindness and asked leave to go to the ball again the next evening, as the prince had specially asked her to come. At this same moment there was a loud knock at the door. The faery and Cinderella's beautiful clothes vanished, and she drew back the bolt to let her stepmother and stepsisters in.

Cinderella's stepsisters told her of the beautiful and unknown princess who had been at the ball. The next day, Cinderella spent the whole day helping her stepsisters get ready for the ball. When they left, her faery Goddess-Mother suddenly appeared, and Cinderella went too in her coach, even more beautifully dressed than before. The prince again remained beside her, danced every dance with her, and said so many kind and loving things to her, that Cinderella, in her happiness, forgot how quickly the hours flew past.

She thought it not yet 11 p.m., when the clock struck midnight. She bolted from the great hall as swiftly as a doe. The prince sped after her, but he couldn't catch up with her. The only trace of Cinderella was her little glass slipper lying on the staircase.

The next morning the countryside was roused by a sound of trumpets. Over the roads and through the streets of town came the royal chamberlain, with guards and an attendant carrying the glass slipper on a green velvet cushion. They stopped at every house and asked each young woman to try on the slipper in an effort to find the beautiful and unknown princess.

Cinderella's stepsisters were in great haste to try on the slipper. Even though they pinched their toes and squeezed their heels, their feet were far too large to go into the shoe. The royal chamberlain enquired whether there were any other young women in the house.

"Only Cinderella," said the elder sister. "And of course the slipper would not fit her."

"Let her be brought here," requested the chamberlain. So, Cinderella was sent for, and, sitting down in the chair, the royal chamberlain put the slipper on Cinderella's foot. It fit perfectly. Then, to the surprise of everyone, Cinderella drew the other little glass slipper from her pocket, and also put it on. At the same moment, the faery Goddess-Mother appeared. With a touch of her magick wand, Cinderella's poor garments transformed into fine robes more splendid than ever.

Everyone saw that Cinderella was indeed the beautiful princess whom the prince loved. Then her stepmother and stepsisters fell at Cinderella's feet and begged her forgiveness. She freely forgave them, and then accompanied the chamberlain to the palace. The prince rushed to meet her with great joy. They were married the same day. Soon afterwards, Cinderella fetched her stepsisters to live at the palace. And they were so much ashamed of their past conduct, and so grateful for her kindness, that they ceased to be proud and unkind. As their hearts became kind, their faces became beautiful. Then two lords of the court loved and married them, and they, as well as Cinderella, lived happily ever after.

The story of Cinderella is one that most of us are familiar with. (This particular one, *The Glass Slipper*, was adapted from a version from M.A. Donohue and Co., in 1912.) You may not have your own faery Goddess-Mother with a magick wand to help you as Cinderella did, but empowerment is all that much easier when you do enlist the helpful powers of the faeries. To enlist their aid, you first need to attract and communicate with them. The following spells are designed to do just that.

Faery Fountain Empowerment

Planting flowers and herbs such as honeysuckle, yarrow, lilac, red valerian, thyme, heliotrope, and daisies, as well as roses, cosmos, petunias, pansies, lavender, and rosemary, are certain to please and attract the flower faeries and butterflies, bees, and hummingbirds. One sure way to draw the helpful Water faeries to you is by putting a fountain in your garden or setting up a tabletop fountain in your home or office.

   * A fountain (garden or tabletop).
   * A glass of milk.
   * A stone with a Natural-bored hole in it.

   1. An hour before sunrise, sit in front of your fountain. Take a few deep breaths to center yourself. Then draw a Faery Ring around the garden area or room. Draw a Faery Magick Circle and then call in the faery guardians.

   2. Now hold the glass of milk up as if to toast, and say:

   *"To the helpful and friendly Water fae
   Bless you today and every day!"*

Drink half of the milk, and then pour the other half into the Earth as an offering to the Water faeries. As you do this, repeat:

   *"To the helpful and friendly Water fae
   Bless you today and every day!"*

   3. Next, hold the stone in your power hand, and face the North point of your Circle. Merge with the Water faeries of the North, hold the stone up to your left eye and look through it. One of the best ways to see the faeries is to look through a Naturally-bored hole in a stone. (Note: You can usually find one of these by the seashore, river, or a waterfall.) Remember to steadily gaze at the faeries when you see them. If you blink, the faeries will vanish. As you gaze through the hole in the stone, say:

   *"Helpful and friendly Water fae of the North
   Please, show yourselves to me.
   I ask for your blessing and protection
   Every night and every day.
   May my mind flow with creativity,*

May my body flow with well-being,
May my spirit flow with grace
By the helpful and friendly fae,
So be it! Blessed be!"

4. Now, face the East point of your Circle, and merge with the Water faeries of the East. Look through the hole in the stone, and say:

"Helpful and friendly Water fae of the East
Please, show yourselves to me.
I ask for your blessing and protection
Every night and every day
May my mind flow with creativity,
May my body flow with well-being,
May my spirit flow with grace
By the helpful and friendly fae,
So be it! Blessed be!"

5. Then, face the South point of your Circle, and merge with the Water faeries of the South. Once again, gaze through the hole in the stone with your left eye, and say:

"Helpful and friendly Water fae of the South
Please, show yourselves to me.
I ask for your blessing and protection
Every night and every day.
May my mind flow with creativity,
May my body flow with well-being,
May my spirit flow with grace.
By the helpful and friendly fae,
So be it! Blessed be!"

6. Next, face the West point of your Circle, and merge with the Water faeries of the West. Gaze through the hole in the stone, and say:

"Helpful and friendly Water fae of the West
Please, show yourselves to me.

I ask for your blessing and protection
Every night and every day.
May my mind flow with creativity,
May my body flow with well-being,
May my spirit flow with grace.
By the helpful and friendly fae,
So be it! Blessed be!"

7. Place the stone next to or in your fountain to attract the helpful powers of the Water fae from North, East, South, and West.

8. When you are done, thank the Water faeries, bid farewell to the faery guardians, and pull up your Faery Circle and Ring.

Rose-Planting Spell

The fragrance of roses acts as a powerful faery attracting force. Use this spell to bring the helpful rose faeries into your garden. Then watch your life blossom with positive magick and joy.

+ A young rose bush
+ A sharp rock
+ Water

1. Draw a Faery Ring and Circle around the area you are planting the rose bush in. Call in the faery guardians.

2. Then dig the proper sized hole to plant the bush in with the sharp stone.

3. Plant your young rose bush in the ground. As you plant the bush, chant:

"By the powers of the flowering fae
Bless this beautiful young rose today."

4. After you are done planting the rose, walk clockwise (sunwise) around the bush three times, and say:

> *"Gather round dear faeries of the rose*
> *Come and watch over this young rose.*
> *Help her grow and leaf and flower,*
> *Guard and teach this beautiful flower,*
> *Each day and every minute of the hour,*
> *By the powers of North, East, South, and West.*
> *In the name of fae, may this rose-child be blessed!"*

5. Water the young bush, and walk around it clockwise three more times. Then repeat:

> *"Gather round dear faeries of the rose*
> *Come and watch over this young rose.*
> *Help her grow and leaf and flower,*
> *Guard and teach this beautiful flower,*
> *Each day and every minute of the hour,*
> *By the powers of North, East, South, and West.*
> *In the name of fae, may this rose-child be blessed!"*

6. Walk three more times clockwise around the bush, and repeat a third time:

> *"Gather round dear faeries of the rose*
> *Come and watch over this young rose.*
> *Help her grow and leaf and flower,*
> *Guard and teach this beautiful flower,*
> *Each day and every minute of the hour,*
> *By the powers of North, East, South, and West.*
> *In the name of fae, may this rose-child be blessed!"*

7. Each and every day, tend to and make sure the bush gets enough water to thrive and blossom. As you do this, chant:

> *"By the powers of the flowering fae*
> *Bless this beautiful rose today and every day."*

8. When you are done, thank the flowers fae, and pull up your Circle.

Respect Your Elders Creativity Spell

A symbol of abundance, creativity, and realizing your full potential, the elder tree is also referred to as the "Thirteenth Tree" because of its close connection with the fae and magick-making. Elder tree stems are used to make panpipes, a faery favorite, and the flowers are ideal for Wish Magick. The elder is a sacred blessing and protection tree of the faeries, and sleeping beneath an elder on a full moon or Sabbat helps you see faery queens and kings.

+ An elder, birch, or oak tree.
+ A hand-held mirror.
+ Apricot oil.
+ A compass.
+ A full moon in the summertime.

1. At dusk, on a warm summer night of a full moon, take the mirror, compass, and apricot oil and go outside and find an elder, birch, or oak tree. Draw a Faery Ring around the tree with your heel, and then drop several drops of the apricot oil clockwise around the ring. Then, draw a Faery Magick Circle and call in the faery guardians.

2. Take a few moments to center yourself. Next, hold the oil in your hands for several minutes to warm it up. Hold the oil between your hands as if to pray, and take a deep breath in, hold your breath for a few seconds, and then pulse your breath out sharply through your nose. As you pulse your breath out, with your intention and thought energy, imagine planting the image of expanded creativity

and abundance into the oil itself. Repeat this process a total of three times to fully charge the oil with the powers of creativity and abundance.

3. Use the compass to determine the East side of the tree trunk. Stand and face the East side of the tree, and say three times:

"By the sacred powers of the standing trees
Bu ba bi be bo, please empower my creativity!"

Then use the oil to trace the "B" (ᛒ) Berkana (pronounced Bur-kan-a) rune on the East face of the tree trunk nine times. As you do this chant:

"Berkana, Berkana, Berkana,
Berkana, Berkana, Berkana,
Berkana, Berkana, Berkana,
Bu ba bi be bo, blessed be!"

4. Now, trace the Berkana rune nine times on each of your palms, one palm at a time. Each time you draw the rune, say the rune's name aloud:

"Berkana"

Next, gently and respectfully place both your palms on the East face of the tree trunk, and repeat three times:

"By the sacred powers of the standing trees
Bu ba bi be bo, please empower my creativity!"

Continue to touch the tree, and repeat once more:

"Berkana, Berkana, Berkana,
Berkana, Berkana, Berkana,
Berkana, Berkana, Berkana,
Bu ba bi be bo, blessed be!"

5. Now turn around and face West. Hold the mirror in your hand, so you can see your face and the East face of the tree trunk in the glass. To connect with and see the faeries is to merge with the reflection of Earth. Look at yourself

and the tree in the mirror. Imagine stepping into that mirror now, and say three times:

> *"By the sacred powers of the standing trees*
> *Bu ba bi be bo, please empower my creativity!"*

6. Sit beneath the tree (with your body making contact with it in some way) for at least 30 minutes. As you do, imagine your creativity and abundance expanding three-fold, then nine-fold, then 18-fold, 100-fold, and even more. See and sense yourself realizing your full potential. Enjoy the image and sensations as you relax beneath the sacred tree.

7. When you are done, thank the tree spirits, bid farewell to the faery guardians, and pull up the Circle and Ring.

Faery Power Dream Bag

This dream bag is designed to help you attain your personal goals by communicating with the helpful and friendly flower faeries in your dreams. As you sleep, the pressure of your head releases the magickal fragrance of the flowers and encourages empowering faery dreams.

- Soft music.
- A gold or silver drawstring bag.
- 1/4 cup dried rose petals.
- 1/4 cup dried lavender flowers.
- 1/4 cup dried jasmine flowers.
- 1/4 cup dried daisies.
- Honeysuckle-scented oil.

1. Turn on some soft music to work by. Stuff the flowers into the drawstring bag. As you do this, chant:

> *"Magickal flower faery dreams, come to me."*

2. Pour several drops of the honeysuckle oil onto the flowers. As you do, repeat:

"Magickal flower faery dreams, come to me."

3. Now close the bag by pulling the drawstring tight. As you tie the drawstring, once again repeat:

"Magickal flower faery dreams, come to me."

4. Put the Dream Empowerment Bag inside your pillowcase. Play the soft music you played when you were making the empowerment bag as you go to sleep. As you drift to sleep, repeat to yourself:

"Magickal flower faery dreams, come to me."

5. Keep the dream bag in your pillowcase for three months to encourage magickal faery dreams. Make a note of these dreams as you recall them.

6. After three months, pour the contents back into the earth under a flower bush as an offering to the flower faeries.

Winged Message Spell

This Winged Message Spell enlists the help of the winged faeries such as butterflies, bees, and birds to help you answer a pressing question about a goal you are manifesting right now.

+ A garden, backyard, or park.

+ 9 pinches of sage.

+ 9 pinches of vervain.

+ Bits of bread and seed corn.

+ A compass.

+ Your Faery Magick journal and pen.

1. Go into Nature at 9 a.m. Stand facing East, and take a few deep breaths. Then draw a Faery Ring, starting at the

Eastern point, and scatter the sage and vervain clockwise around the outside of the Ring. Now, scatter the bits of bread and seed corn around the inside of the Ring.

2. Next, draw a Faery Magick Circle, starting at the East point, and call in the faery guardians.

3. Now face East, close your eyes, and think of one question about a goal you are manifesting. Keep focused on that one question, and then open your eyes. Use the compass to note from what direction the first bird, bee, butterfly, or other insect flies toward you. If the first winged messenger comes from the East, it indicates a positive response to your question and much personal success with regards to your question. If the winged messenger comes from the South, it means you need to apply more personal power and creativity to the question at hand. If the winged messenger comes from the West, it means you will be successful in attaining your goal. If the winged messenger comes from the North, it indicates a negative response to your question.

4. Make a note of the direction of the first winged messenger in your Faery Magick journal.

5. When you are done, thank the winged faeries, bid farewell to the faery guardians, and pull up your Circle and Ring. You can repeat this spell as often as you like.

Faery Empowerment Charm

Have you ever needed just a little more power to get you over that next hurdle when manifesting your deepest dreams? This Faery Acorn Empowerment talisman with staurolite is tailor-made to help you leap those hurdles and make your dreams come true! Staurolite is a mineral that grows in the form of flat crystals that form a Natural faery cross. Make this talisman indoors an hour before sunrise on one of the eight Sabbats for best results.

+ Two oak leaves.
+ White rose petals.
+ A white candle.
+ A red pouch.
+ An acorn.
+ A piece of staurolite.
+ 3 pinches of rosemary.
+ 3 pinches of lavender.
+ 9 inches of green ribbon.
+ 1/2 cup of spring or well water.

1. First, put the oak leaves in your shoes, and put your shoes on your feet. Then draw a Faery Ring, and scatter the white rose petals clockwise just inside the outline of the Ring. Next, draw a Faery Magick Circle, and call in the faery guardians.

2. Light the candle, and dedicate it to the helpful faeries. Say:

"I dedicate this candle to the helpful faeries."

3. Put the staurolite in your mouth for a few minutes. This attunes it to your personal energy field.

4. Next, anoint the staurolite with the water. As you do, say:

"I consecrate and empower this stone
With the magickal powers of the faeries.
As above, so below. So be it! Blessed be!"

5. Anoint the acorn with the water. As you do, say:

"I consecrate and empower this acorn
With the magickal powers of the faeries.
As above, so below. So be it! Blessed be!"

6. Put the stone, acorn, rosemary, lavender, and ribbon into the red pouch. Sprinkle the pouch with water, and then hold it in your hands and say:

"I consecrate and empower this charm
With the magickal powers of the faeries.
As above, so below. So be it! Blessed be!"

7. After you are done, thank the helpful faeries, bid fare-well to the faery guardians, and pull up the Circle. Allow the candle to safely burn down. Carry or hold the pouch in your hands to encourage faery sightings and communications.

Faery Queen Power Spell

One of the most well-known faery queens is Titania. Her name is the title of Mother Earth as the source of all the gigantic Titans. Over time, the faeries shrank in size, and went from being larger than life, to smaller than mortals. This spell enlists the helpful power of the mighty faery queens such as Titania to attain your goals and enrich your life.

+   A gold ring.
+   A bell.
+   Yellow roses.
+   A cup of white confectioner's sugar.
+   3 Tbs. pure vanilla extract.
+   Wax paper.

1. Draw a Faery Ring, and scatter the yellow roses clockwise around it. Then draw a Faery Magick Circle and call in the faery guardians.

2. Next, spread the sugar on wax paper and sprinkle it with vanilla. Thoroughly mix the vanilla into the sugar. Set this aside.

3. Now ring the bell seven times, and say:

"Beautiful and blessed faery queens,
Please help and empower me,

Enrich my life with your power,
Every second, minute, and each hour.
By the faery Ladies, blessed be!"

4. Then put on the gold ring on your receiving hand (your left hand if you are right-handed). Hold your hand with the ring upward, and repeat:

"Beautiful and blessed faery queens,
Please help and empower me,
Enrich my life with your power,
Every second, minute, and each hour.
By the faery Ladies, blessed be!"

5. Now cut an energy door, and go outdoors with the wax paper and sugar. Sprinkle the sugar on the earth, and repeat:

"Beautiful and blessed faery queens,
Please help and empower me,
Enrich my life with your power,
Every second, minute, and each hour.
By the faery Ladies, blessed be!"

6. When you are done, go back inside, thank the faery queens, bid farewell to the faery guardians, and pull up your Circle and Ring.

7. Wear the ring to draw the enriching and empowering energies of the faery queens into your life, every second, minute, and each hour.

Faery Name Spell

Names are magickal as well as powerful. Your magickal faery name represents your faery self. Use this name when doing magick. As you use the name again and again during spellwork and meditation, its creative, magickal power will unfold within you. For best results, do this work one hour before sunrise or at dusk on a full moon.

+ A green votive candle.

+ Your Faery Magick journal and pen.

+ Lavender oil.

1. Begin by drawing a Faery Ring and Circle around your altar area. Then, call in the faery guardians.

2. Next, rub a thin film of lavender oil on the candle and put it in its holder on your altar. Anoint yourself with the oil. Wipe the oil from your hands, light the candle, and say:

"In this bright flame
Illuminate my faery name."

3. Sit or recline comfortably where you can easily see the candle flame. Focus your awareness on the flame as you breathe in for three heartbeats, still your breath for three heartbeats, and exhale for three heartbeats. Do this three times. As you exhale, let go of any tension and stress you may be feeling. Keep gazing at the candle flame and breathing rhythmically, allowing yourself to relax more and more.

4. As you breathe in, imagine you are breathing in a bright green light into your body. Imagine your being filling with bright green light, and as you breathe out, imagine the light surrounding you in all directions, above and below, like a large egg. Do this three times as you continue to focus on the flame.

5. Next, imagine magickally stepping into the flame and communicating with the faeries. Say aloud three times:

"Helpful fae, blessed be
Reveal my faery name to me."

6. Take a few moments and make a note in your journal of the names that come to mind. Hone in on the one name that feels right to you. Often, it's the name that has creates the strongest positive response within you. It may be a traditional

faery name, a word, an animal, or flower name, or a word or name you aren't familiar with.

7. Once you know your faery name, write it down on a separate page in your journal and also note the date and time. Strengthen the power of your faery name by saying three times:

> *"I am (state your faery name).*
> *I am the sacred fae of the flame*
> *I am empowered by my magickal name.*
> *So be it! Blessed be!"*

8. Allow the candle to safely burn down. As you drift to sleep, silently repeat your faery name over and over again.

9. In the morning, thank the helpful faeries, bid farewell to the faery guardians, and pull up the Circle and Ring.

Bibliography

Anderson, Rosemarie. *Celtic Oracles*. New York: Harmony Books, 1998.

Baumgartner, Anne. *A Comprehensive Dictionary of the Gods*. New York: University Books, 1984.

Bonwick, James. *Irish Druids and Old Irish Religions*. New York: Dorset, 1986.

Bowes, Susan. *Notions and Potions*. New York: Sterling Publishing Co., Inc., 1997.

Bord, Janet and Colin Bord. *Mysterious Britain*. London: Paladin Books, 1974.

Briggs, K.M. *The Fairies in English Tradition and Literature*. Chicago, IL: University of Chicago Press, 1967.

Cabarga, Leslie. *Talks With Trees*. Los Angeles, CA: Iconoclassics Publishing Co., 1997.

Cleary, Rhondda. *Fragrant Candles*. New South Wales, Australia: Sally Milner Publishing, 1997.

Coffey, Lisa Marie. *Getting There With Grace*. Boston, MA: Journey Editions, 2001.

Creasy, Rosalind. *The Edible Herb Garden*. Boston, MA: Periplus Editions, 1999.

Currot, Phyllis. *WitchCrafting*. New York: Broadway Books, 2001.

Darling, Benjamin. *Shakespeare on Fairies and Magic.* Paramus, NJ: Prentice Hall, 2001.

Del Ray, Lester, and Risa Kessler (Editors). *Once Upon A Time.* New York: Ballantine Books, 1991.

Diamond, Denise. *Living With Flowers.* New York: William Morrow and Company, 1982.

Eisenkraft-Palazzola, Lori. *Faeries, Doorways to the Enchanted Realm.* New York: Smithmark Publishers, 1999.

Evans-Wentz, W.Y. *The Fairy Faith in Celtic Countries.* New York: Citadel Press, 1990.

Farrar, Janet and Stewart. *A Witches' Bible.* New York: Magical Childe, 1984.

Frazier, Sir James George. *The Golden Bough.* New York: The Macmillan Company, 1935.

Gannon, Linda. *Creating Fairy Garden Fragrances.* Pownal, Vermont: Storey Books, 1998.

Gray, Deborah. *The Good Witch's Guide to Wicked Ways.* Boston, MA: Journey Editions, 2001.

Grimal, Pierre (Editor). *Larousse World Mythology.* London: Paul Hamlyn, 1965.

Jacobs, Joseph (Collected by). *Celtic Fairytales.* New York: Dover Publications, Inc., 1968.

Jacobs, Joseph. *European Folk and Fairy Tales.* New York: G. P. Putnam's Sons, 1916.

Jay, Roni. *Gardens of the Spirit.* New York: Sterling Publishing Co., 1998.

Kluger, Marilyn. *The Wild Flavor.* Los Angeles: Jeremy P. Tarcher Inc., 1984.

Knight, Sirona. *A Witch Like Me.* Franklin Lakes, NJ: New Page Books, 2001.

——. *Celtic Traditions.* New York: Citadel Press, 2000.

———. *Dream Magic: Night Spells and Rituals For Love, Prosperity, and Personal Power.* San Francisco, CA: HarperSanFrancisco, 2000.

———. *Exploring Celtic Druidism.* Franklin Lakes, NJ: New Page Books, 2001.

———. *Goddess Bless.* Red Wheel Publishing, 2002.

———. *The Little Giant Encyclopedia of Runes.* New York: Sterling Publishing Co., 2000.

———. *Love, Sex, and Magick.* New York: Citadel Press, 1999.

———. *The Pocket Guide to Celtic Spirituality.* Freedom, CA: Crossing Press, 1998.

———. *The Pocket Guide to Crystals and Gemstones.* Freedom, CA: Crossing Press, 1998.

———. et al. *The Shapeshifter Tarot.* St. Paul, MN: Llewellyn Publications, 1998.

———. *The Wiccan Spell Kit.* New York: Kensington Books/Citadel Press, 2001.

———. *The Witch and Wizard Training Guide.* New York: Kensington Books/Citadel Press, 2001.

Leach, Maria, Editor. *Standard Dictionary of Folklore, Mythology, and Legend.* New York: Funk & Wagnalls Co., 1950.

Leodhas, Sorche Nic. *Sea-Spell and Moor-Magic.* New York: Holt, Rinehart, and Winston, Inc., 1968.

Long, Jim. *Making Herbal Dream Pillows.* Pownal, Vermont: Storey Books, 1998.

Macnamara, Niall. *Leprehaun Companion.* New York: Barnes & Noble Books, 1999.

MacRitchie, David. *FIans, Fairies, and Picts.* London: Norwood Editions, 1975.

Markale, Jean. *Merlin: Priest of Nature.* Rochester, VT: Inner Traditions, 1995.

Martin, Laura C. *Garden Flower Folklore.* Chester, CN: The Globe Pequot Press, 1987.

Melville, Francis. *Love Potions and Charms.* Hauppauge, NY: Barron's, 2001.

Mercatante, Anthony. *The Magic Garden.* New York: Harper and Row: 1976.

Monaghan, Patricia. *The Book of Goddesses and Heroines.* St. Paul, MN: Llewellyn Publications, 1990.

——. *Magical Gardens.* St. Paul, MN: Llewellyn Publications, 1997.

Morris, Jan. *A Matter of Wales.* Oxford: Oxford University Press, 1984.

Morrison, Dorothy. *Yule.* St. Paul, MN: Llewellyn Publications, 2000.

Nahmad, Claire. *Cat Spells.* London: Parkgate Books, 1998.

Paterson, Helena. *Handbook of Celtic Astrology.* St. Paul, MN: Llewellyn Publications, 1995.

Rees, Alwyn & Brinley. *Celtic Heritage, Ancient Tradition in Ireland and Wales.* New York: Grove Press, 1978.

Rhys, John, M. A. *Celtic Folklore, Welsh and Manx.* New York: Benjamin Blom, Inc., 1972.

Ross, Anne. *Pagan Celtic Britain.* New York: Columbia University Press, 1967.

Scalora, Suza. *The Fairies.* New York: HarperCollins, 1999.

Squire, Charles. *Celtic Myth and Legend.* Franklin Lakes, NJ: New Page Books, 2001.

Starhawk. *The Spiral Dance.* San Francisco, CA: Harper SanFrancisco, 1979.

Stepanich, Kisma. *Faery Wicca, Book One.* St. Paul, MN: Llewellyn Publications, 1994.

——. *Faery Wicca, Book Two.* St. Paul, MN: Llewellyn Publications, 1995.

Stephens, James. *Irish Fairy Tales.* New York: Collier Books, 1962.

Stewart, R.J. *Celtic Gods, Celtic Goddesses.* New York: Sterling Publishing Co., 1990.

——. *Earth Light.* Rockport, MA: Element Books, 1992.

——. *The Living World of Faery.* Glastonbury, Somerset: Gothic Image Publication, 1995.

——. *The Power Within the Land.* Rockport, MA: Element Books, 1992.

Telesco, Patricia. *Money Magick.* Franklin Lakes, NJ: New Page Books, 2001.

Weinstein, Marion. *Earth Magic.* New York: Earth Magic Productions, 1998.

Wilde, Lady. *Ancient Legends, Mystic Charms and Superstitions of Ireland.* New York: Lemma Publishing, 1973.

Worwood, Valerie. *The Complete Book of Essential Oils and Aromatherapy.* New York: New World Library, 1995.

Yeats, W.B., Editor. *Fairy & Folk Tales of Ireland.* New York: Macmillan Publishing Co., 1983.

Index

A

T

U

W

Y